50 Short Climbs in the Midwest

50 Short Climbs in the Midwest

Alan Bagg

Produced by Greatlakes Living Press
of Waukegan, Illinois,
for Contemporary Books, Inc.

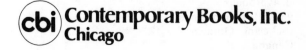 Contemporary Books, Inc.
Chicago

Library of Congress Cataloging in Publication Data

Bagg, Alan.
  Fifty Short Climbs in the Midwest.

  Includes bibliographical references and index.
  1. Rock climbing—Middle West—Guide-books.
2. Middle West—Description and travel—Guide-books. I. Title.
GV199.42.M53B33   796.5′22′0977   77-91194
ISBN 0-8092-7668-2
ISBN 0-8092-7667-4 pbk.

Copyright © 1978 by Alan Bagg
All rights reserved
Published by Contemporary Books, Inc.
180 North Michigan Avenue, Chicago, Illinois 60601
Manufactured in the United States of America
Library of Congress Catalog Card Number: 77-91194
International Standard Book Number: 0-8092-7668-2 (cloth)
                    0-8092-7667-4 (paper)

Published simultaneously in Canada by
Beaverbooks
953 Dillingham Road
Pickering, Ontario LlW 1Z7
Canada

Contents

Part 3

Introduction:

Finding a New High

Believe it or not, there are some "mountains" to climb in the flat Midwest—and this book is written for those who seek them out for technical rock climbing. Of course, the climbing areas are not as famous as Yosemite and others out West that have already become popular through climbing literature. But the rock faces ideally suited for rock climbing in the Midwest are often every bit as well known to hard-core climbing addicts. This volume is aimed at the not-so-ardent rock climber: the beginner or intermediate climber who has tested his or her mettle on a few escarpments and would now like to do more varied climbing without the accompanying long-distance trip to the Rockies in the West or the Appalachian faces in the East.

The book is ideal for the weekender in search of a challenging new experience. Hundreds of people, especially college students, have become aware of the recreational value of a weekend climb, as demonstrated by the thriving memberships in college climbing clubs like the University of Wisconsin Hoofers and the climbing clubs at Iowa and Iowa State.

As R.C. Aleith explains in his book *Bergsteigen: Basic Rock Climbing,* "The summit is not always the final goal, nor is the highest peak the greatest challenge. The manner in which the climb is accomplished is often more important to the climber than the . . . peak bagged."

While some elitist climbers might turn up their noses at the scrambling done in the Midwest, by definition, you are climbing when it becomes necessary to use your hands for assistance in moving over a rocky incline. When using a means of protection or equipment for assistance, you are engaged in technical climbing, for which certain techniques are necessary. Your ability to climb is based on the knowledge and practice of those techniques.

Since it is so rudimentary to climbing, a brief introduction to basic equipment appears in Part I with special emphasis given to items of significance to Midwest climbers. Here, too, the beginning climber new to the nomenclature of technical rock climbing is introduced to the Sierra Club's climbing classification (which is used to label the climbs in Part II), as well as geological terminology for the physical aspects of the terrain the climber normally encounters.

A separate chapter devoted to buying necessary equipment and aimed primarily at the beginner who may have none emphasizes the qualities to look for in climbing gear: a brief consumer's guide on boots, clothing, hard hats, and miscellaneous items, as well as ropes, slings, carabiners, and pitons.

Basic climbing techniques will not be discussed since this type of instruction book is readily available. An annotated bibliography of these books is included in a separate chapter in Part 3. It is a recommended reading list of the best of many books and pamphlets written on climbing dealing with techniques and how to upgrade one's climbing skills.

The real heart of *Fifty Short Climbs in the Midwest* is found in Part II: a detailed guide to fifty climbs that range from a few hours to a full day in length in Illinois, Iowa, Michigan, Minnesota, Ohio, and Wisconsin. Information on these climbs includes how to get there, which U.S. Geological Survey quadrangle covers the area, camping facilities nearby, a map and information on the type and difficulty of the rock structure, a suggested route and highlights that make the particular climb unique, and a graded difficulty rating.

Part III also contains chapters which list data on climbing schools in the Midwest (as well as elsewhere in the United States) and local climbing clubs in the Midwest, including a thumbnail sketch of each.

This guidebook borrows heavily on the specific works of many other climbers who have often written about the routes in much greater detail, in other much shorter works. Wherever possible, I have listed the places where the booklets, pamphlets, or guides still in print and available to the public can be acquired. The prices given are at the time of this writing and subject to change. Although varying greatly in quality and quantity of information, the individual guidebooks are recommended as substantial sources of specific information on particular climb sites, usually going into much greater details pertinent to the climbs in that area than can be included in a comprehensive guidebook such as this one. These individual guidebooks also give the flavor of the particular climb sites and often contain attempts at humor that is peculiar to climbing guides.

A wave of antiguidebook feelings runs through the

ranks of climbers in the Midwest (and elsewhere in the country). These opinions have grown in the past few years as a result of the popularity of climbing as a sport. The concept tenaciously held by some of the more hard-bitten elitists is that a guidebook ruins an area because a new ground swell of inexperienced and poorly trained climbers with "no business on the slopes" and "a guidebook mentality and knowledge of climbing" litter and damage the ecology through over-use of certain trails and routes, and are involved in accidents that generally besmirch the name of climbing.

While not dismissing the impact of guidebooks, other factors, including increased leisure time, climbing schools, college clubs, organized outings, mass-media publicity, and the new interest in ecology, have speeded the influx of people to rock scrambling and climbing.

Thus, there are sections of the Midwest where information on new ascents and climbing areas is still privy to an elite few. They discovered them and are rightfully guarding their secrets. Part of the fun of climbing is discovering new routes so there is that challenge left ahead. Other areas and routes printed here are probably listed for the first time anywhere, which will no doubt stir the ire of some and open new vistas for many new, searching climbers.

It is best to recognize that our increased impact on an everexpanding society of climbers and ecology of the individual areas requires a careful approach and concern for everyone involved. It is important to sub-scribe wholeheartedly to the " pack-in, pack-out" ethic of leaving no litter and taking out what you bring in. I'm amazed at the large number of beer cans and candy wrappers stuffed into rock cracks of the more popular sites I've visited. I have no doubt that many were put there by nonclimbing hikers, however.

Accidents can be avoided by learning correct climbing techniques during properly supervised training sessions. The climbing schools and instructional classes of area clubs are listed in this book so that novices and inexperienced climbers can learn the fundamental techniques of climbing quickly and efficiently. The high number of accidents to skilled climbers who tackle summits more advanced than their climbing abilities will no doubt close some climbing areas in the future. It behooves each climber to guard against such occurrences.

Climbers, by their own nature and the nature of the sport, are free spirits who don't want to be constricted by lists of do's and don'ts, but some standard of behavior must prevail among climbers as more and more swell our ranks. If not, the baby will go out with the bath water. Some state governing agencies are already closing areas (Indiana and Illinois, for example) because the risk of accident is too high or the user impact on the ecology of the area is too great. Others threaten to follow suit if climbers can't police their own ranks.

There are no easy answers to the problems. The only solution is for each climber to subscribe to his or her own high standard of conduct and to learn a new set of ethics that apply to the environment and the emerging society of climbers. Royal Robbins sets forth a number of etiquette-type considerations in his *Basic Rockcraft* and *Advanced Rockcraft* books, which should be heeded by all climbers.

It is important to realize the impact of hammering a piton or drilling a bolt hole. In most areas, pitons and, most surely, bolts are openly held in disdain, since they ruin the rocks, thus degrading the climb and all who follow. Even in celebrated Yosemite Valley, clean climbing (no pitons) is now popular, challenging climbers to go completely free or use chocks instead of pitons for protection. Besides saving the rock, nuts or chocks offer a fast, quiet, and more challenging alternative to pitons, and the climber needn't carry a hammer.

Clean climbers have come of age, fulfilling their progress with increased finesse instead of forcing more protection, relying less on technology and more on technique and skill. Throughout the Midwest, this trend is obvious. But even so, still another problem pops up: chalk dust plastered even on simpler climbs, mapping the routes as if they were paint-by-numbers canvas boards.

These are some of the ethical considerations that will have to be reckoned with as the sport develops during the next few years. All we can do to preserve it is to clean up our own act.

50
Short
Climbs
in the
Midwest

part 1

1

Coming to Terms with Technical Rock Climbing

Climbing has its own unique vocabulary, which is often baffling to the beginner. There are new words for geological features or terrain such as slab, chimney, col, and jam crack; terms for technique such as laybacking, friction, and belay; terms for equipment such as brake bar, carabiner, and RURP; and even terms to describe the difficulty of the climb.

A more formal glossary of terms follows the main text of this book and includes vocabulary which may be confusing to beginning and/or intermediate climbers. This chapter presents a discussion on climbing classifications and a list of important climbing calls which every climber must know to participate safely in the sport.

Climbers have found it desirable to convey the difficulty of a climb by referring to a standard rating system. The same objective exists among the several systems that have developed: to evaluate the climbing routes by a simple, universally recognized classification.

Climbing ratings are normally subjects of great debate and, of course, open to human error, but most climbers find them helpful in selecting routes within their known range of ability, so the ratings are a standard part of the climber's vocabulary.

Modified Sierra Club Classification

Class 1 is simply walking upright—hiking without the use of hands and special footwear.

Class 2 is rock scrambling, often over large blocks of rock using hands to balance and appropriate rubber-soled shoes. Small leaps must often be made between large boulders.

Class 3 is easy climbing over somewhat steeper ground than Class 2 and over large rocks using handholds and footholds, usually quite large and easy to locate. Exposure (a term climbers use to describe the feeling or awareness of height and the possibility of falling off the rock) is not enough to demand rope, although beginners might desire one since the route is often easy but frightening, which makes beginners feel quite queasy.

Class 4 involves increased exposure and roped climbing with belaying. Steep rock and much smaller holds could result in a very serious or fatal fall if the climber isn't roped in. Some moves may be difficult and could be Class 5, except for the security of short pitches or natural protection against falls such as trees, shrubs, and rock horns.

Class 5 involves difficult routes with severe exposure making the placement of pitons or other artificial means of protection by the leader somewhat common. This category is subdivided into twelve smaller groupings—5.0 through 5.11. Available holds, often less than an inch wide, must be sought out and chockstones (nuts) and pitons (pins) are sometimes placed for more protection. Techniques like jamming and laybacking are used here.

Class 6 consists of direct aid—climbing where holds or cracks in the rock are not adequate for roped free climbing. Pitons and bolts are used in connection with stirrups and tension. Routes are rated from A1 to A5; A1 being quite easy and A5 requiring difficult and very insecure placements.

While climbers are generally concerned with all the Sierra Club classes of climbs, Classes 5 and 6 are of particular value. Many hikers and adventurers have probably participated in Class 2 and 3 climbing without even being aware of it, but when a climber sets out to apply his craft to the rock, it's a sure bet he or she will be attempting Class 5 and 6. Therefore, a more specific system of categorizing rock surfaces and the over-all route system is needed, and virtually all climbers use a decimal system that more closely describes the amount of difficulty on various parts of the pitch. This add-on decimal system is normally written in full—5.3 or Class 5.3—in guidebooks, but when used in conversation the whole number 5 is normally dropped. So, when a climber says "That's a '7' or '8,'" referring to a particular climb, he means Class 5.7 or 5.8.

In classifying a climb we consider the total climb, not just the vertical pitches. But the value assigned to the whole climb is based on the most difficult move. If the single most difficult move on a climb is 5.8 on only one pitch, it is a Class 5.8 climb. If it also has an A3 aid move, the climb is Class 5.8-A3. Most of the climbs in this book are of only one pitch.

Because climbs are rated by climbers (usually the "resident expert" or first leader of the climb), the system is far from scientific. How the climber felt the day of the climb, his climbing experience, whether the rock was wet or dry, and the particular route used (slab, crack, chimney, etc.) are all factors entering into the decision to assign the climb a certain value. Therefore, individual climbers will argue forever about the rating and each may be right in his or her own way. The classification must therefore be considered as a generally accurate consensus of the difficulty of the climb so that all climbers work with the same language.

For this reason, it is good to remember when using this guidebook or any guidebook that route selection should be based on your acknowledged ability, but that there is considerable latitude in guidebook descriptions (for the above mentioned reasons) and standards vary from one climbing area to another.

With the constant upgrading of equipment and skills, the climbs listed here will generally get easier; but because of increased standards, the converse is sometimes true.

Another consideration is that skill on one type of rock often translates poorly to another. For instance, a good granite crack climber may have much difficulty on a sandstone slab. Accustomed to the relative security of fingers and toes jammed in a crack, he may find little comfort in the assurances of his partner that the super friction of a coarse-grained, high-angle slab offers abundant security. Therefore, climbing problems must always be evaluated locally. Geographic location, season, type of rock, present weather, and local weather patterns, all combine to create problems peculiar to each region.

There is also another classification system called the National Climbing Classification System (NCCS) which was developed in 1963 to provide a more specific nation-wide classification based on three separate elements: grade—total effort involved in the climb (time and distance), type—aid or free, and class—a designation for the most difficult portion of the climb which corresponds to the Sierra Club system.

Throughout this book only a modified NCCS system will be used, since it is universally recognized by Midwestern climbers as well as by those in other parts of the country and Canada. It is also good to keep in mind that virtually all Midwestern climbing involves no mountaineering skills which add to the over-all difficulty of climbing. Therefore, for the sake of simplicity all climbs unless preceded by another roman numeral, will be assumed to be Grade I. Thus, the term "Grade" should not be confused with "Class," which evaluates only the technical climbing difficulty. Furthermore, mastering the art of Class 5.8 moves on lowland boulders will not assure success on a difficult alpine ascent in the West. For example, a Class 5.7 or 5.8 practice climb on boulders or cliffs next to the highway might be only Grade I, while a remote alpine cliff of the same technical difficulty may be Grade IV or V if it is necessary to do eighteen rope leads of sustained Class 4 and 5 to get to it. Therefore, to put into perspective the differences in true mountaineering versus the technical climbing done by day-tripping Midwesterners, the following system is noted:

Grade I: Technical portions can be done in several hours.

Grade II: Technical portions require half a day.

Grade III: Technical portions require most of a day. (A minimum pitch difficulty need not be specified for Grades I, II, and III.)

Grade IV: Requires one long day; the hardest pitch is rarely less than Class 5.7.

Grade V: Requires 1½ to 2½ days; the hardest pitch is rarely less than Class 5.8.

Grade VI: Usually requires two or more days with considerable difficult free and aid climbing.

Climbing Calls

To avoid garbled communications between the climber and his belayer during the climb, a set of climbing calls have been formulated and are tightly adhered to by good climbers. Less formal conversations usually will not work since often the belayer or climber is out of sight of the other, in a position where the casual voice or less than standard calls will not carry. The set call system is short and demands a verifying response from the climber or belayer. If the answer is not returned or is returned in improper sequence, it is obvious the call wasn't understood.

The calls listed here are taken from Aleith's *Bergsteigen: Basic Rock Climbing.*

Rock: A warning given by anyone—climber, belayer, or bystander. The call means something (rock, log, piton, etc.) is falling and people below are possibly in danger of being struck.

Ready: The first call sometimes given by the climber to the belayer when he is ready to start climbing. If he does not receive an answer from the belayer, it may be because the belayer is not ready or has not heard the climber. The climber should not start to climb until the belayer answers.

On Belay: An information call given by the belayer. It means the belayer is ready and able to provide a safe belay for the climber. The call requires no answer.

Testing: A call given by the climber to inform the belayer that the climber desires to test the belay system. This call requires an answer before any action can be initiated.

Test: Given by the belayer in answer to the call "Testing," meaning the belayer is ready for an actual belay system test. It requires no answer;

after hearing this call the climber conducts the test.

Climbing: Given by the climber to notify the belayer he is about to start climbing. The call requires an answer and no action is taken by the climber until he receives one.

Climb: Given by the belayer to notify the climber he may start climbing. The call requires no answer and the actual climbing begins after this call.

Up Rope: Given by the climber to notify the belayer to take up the rope. It is important to the climber that no slack develops in the belay rope. The call requires no answer, just action on the part of the belayer.

Slack: Given by the climber to notify the belayer to let out rope. Slack may be required to make a traverse, negotiate a tricky move, or untangle the belay rope. The call requires no answer, just action by the belayer.

Tension: Given by the climber to notify the belayer to take up as much of the belay rope as his strength will allow. This may be required for a rest stop, a tricky move, or just for the climber's confidence. It requires no answer, only the belayer's action.

Falling: A warning given by the climber to notify the belayer that the climber is falling or that a fall is imminent. The call is given since in many circumstances the belayer cannot feel the fall. It requires no answer, just a safe belay catch. (The exact wording may vary depending upon the climber's mental attitude at the time.)

Off Belay: Given by the climber to notify the belayer that the climber is secure and is ready to remove the belay rope. The call requires an answer before further action can be taken.

Belay Off: Given by the belayer to notify the climber that the safety of the belay rope is about to be removed. After this call, the climber and belayer may either proceed to remove the belay system or prepare to belay the next climber.

Rope: Given as a warning to notify climbers and by-standers that a rope is being thrown. The call requires no answer.

Off Rappel: Given by a rappelling climber to notify the climbers remaining above that he has safely rap-pelled and has completely freed himself of the rappel rope. The call requires no answer, but a climber must not begin to rappel until he has received this call from the previous rappeller.

2

Equipment to Put You "On Belay"

Midwestern climbers need little in the way of equipment. Unlike the vast areas of the Canadian and American West where it might take the better part of a day to trek into the climb site, Midwest sites are nearly all located within easy access of a highway or road and require only a short hike to the climbing area.

Therefore, frame packs, mountaineering boots, bivouac tents, crampons, and other expedition equipment can be dispensed with in favor of a few basic essential pieces of equipment. Not needing the expensive gear makes it easier on the climber's pocketbook and justifies the investment in the best affordable climbing gear. This extra quality of some items is highly worthwhile, especially when considering your very life depends on it, such as in the case of the climbing rope or other items that are part of the protection system.

Clothing is not a prime consideration for climbing in the Midwest either, since the elements are not so severe that you can't beat a quick retreat to your campsite or car or dig into a rucksack for an extra shirt, sweater, or parka.

Boots

It is not necessary to use thick, lug-soled mountaineering boots in the Midwest. Specialized lightweight rock-climbing shoes (known generally as *kletterschuhe*) allow much greater feel for the rock through the thinner soles and aren't as clumsy.

More manufacturers are turning to the French-designed suede boot with a band of rubber along the sides and on the toe and heel. This band allows better friction on the rock in jam cracks and protects the uppers from abrasion. These lighter rock shoes are more suited to the type of climbing done in the Midwestern states.

A rock shoe must fit snugly so it acts as a part of the foot and permits no sliding of the foot within the shoes. A very narrow welt allows body weight to press the foot firmly to the rock and not slide off a small hold. Since the proper fit is so important, take the time to discuss the right fit with a knowledgeable salesperson; this probably precludes buying technical boots from mail-order houses.

Smooth or cleated soles are available. The smooth ones grip better on rough-textured rocks such as sandstone, while cleated shoes are superior on slick rocks such as eroded granite. Cleats also work better when descending grassy slopes or pine needle-strewn hillsides. Medium-hard rubber seems the best compromise between soft rubber, which grips well but wears quickly and bends badly on small edges, and hard rubber, which doesn't allow as much "feel" for the rock.

The shoes' flexibility is another prime consideration. Stiff soles make it easier to stand on small holds and are better suited for jam cracks than thinner-soled, more flexible shoes, which are superior for holding in rounded holds or on slabs, as well as very narrow jam cracks. The flexible shoe should fit like a glove. The major advantage of this shoe is that it is lighter and usually less expensive than a stiffer one, which consists of more materials.

The stiffer shoe has the advantage of providing better wedge action in most jam cracks while being easier on the toes. It also has more support for standing in slings when aid climbing. Longer wearing shoes should be resoled. This should be an option in the shoes you buy. You can expect to pay $60 or more for a well-manufactured climbing boot.

Rope

The rope is literally the climber's lifeline—protection when his or her strength, judgment, or terrain fail. Therefore, much thought should govern its selection, care, and use.

Today, only synthetic-fiber ropes, such as nylon and perlon, are worth trusting one's life to. Manila and other natural fibers used in the past don't have the comparable qualities of strength and shock absorbency essential for a climbing rope and should not be used as one under any circumstance.

Both strength and elasticity are an inherent part of the construction and materials of the rope. Far more flexible and less susceptible to abrasion than any other rope of its size and weight, the climbing rope is composed of continuous strands which extend from one end to the other, in either a twisted or core-and-sheath construction.

In the time-honored twisted method, three or four

major strands are entwined around each other, forming a less expensive rope than the core-and-sheath-constructed rope. The twisted rope is easily inspected for damage by twisting apart the strands to see the interior.

The core-and-sheath construction is called "kernmantle." Here a core of twisted, braided, or parallel-continuous strands is enclosed in a tightly woven sheath, providing a rope that slides with less friction over rock surfaces or through carabiners, thus eliminating rope drag. With a kernmantle rope it is much more difficult to assess damage, since the interior strands may be broken without the sheath being severed.

Most kernmantles sold in this country are made in Europe. The Union Internationale des Associations d'Alpinisme (UIAA) tests them and assigns a label which guarantees that a rope is safe to be used for climbing (but not necessarily that the rope has the best climbing characteristics, which will be discussed later).

Strong enough to withstand a fall, even after considerable use, the rope must stretch to absorb kinetic energy generated by a fall, but not be so elastic that the climber falls farther or be elastic under static body weight. The average test capability of a climbing rope ranges from three thousand to six thousand pounds. This seemingly extreme capacity is necessary when we consider that the static weight of a 175-pound climber increases to 4,375 pounds of force released on impact at the end of the fall, when the fall is only 25 feet in distance.

According to the formula that states that the approximate weight of the climber multiplied by the number of feet of the fall equals the shock force exerted on the rope, one can see that a 200-pound person falling 25 feet would exert 5,000 pounds of force on the climbing rope.

The climbing rope is the climber's lifeline. Much thought should go into its selection. These kernmantle ropes are most widely used by climbers today. *(Forrest Mountaineering)*

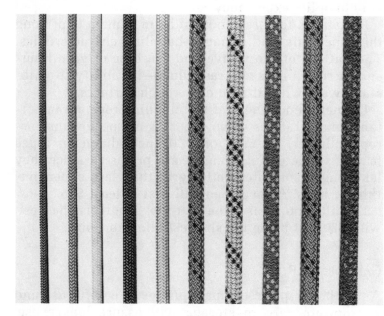

Kernmantle ropes come in a variety of diameters. Those pictured here are from 4 mm. (smallest) to 11 mm. (thickest). For the one-rope climber, 11 mm. is preferred since it lasts longer and offers better grips. An 11 mm. x 150-ft. rope costs about $75. *(Forrest Mountaineering)*.

A rope's behavior in the hand during climbing is determined by its handling characteristics. These characteristics include such things as flexibility, feel, grip, smoothness, and "knotability." A too stiff rope will not hold knots well and will create undue friction when going through several carabiners. One that is too soft will not hold knóts well either. It may also deform, flatten, and sometimes jam when rolling over a pulley. And, because of its limpness, the rope can tie itself up in knots when throwing down a coil. Therefore, a desirable climbing rope is relatively lightweight and abrasion resistant, holds knots well without kinking, produces low friction when passing over rocks or through carabiners, offers good grip to the hands, soaks up little or no water, and has a reasonably long life expectancy.

Resistance to abrasion must be maximum to prolong the rope's life and enhance handling characteristics. The pattern of the weave and the type of yarn influence a rope's abrasion resistance—its ability to withstand wear when drawn over rough surfaces.

Diameter and length of the climbing rope are important considerations when choosing a rope. For the one-rope climber, 11-mm. or 7/16-inch diameter ropes (called single or full-weight) are preferred since they last longer and offer better grip than less expensive, thinner lines. A good rope will cost at least $75.

For all-around use, the 150-foot length is the best, with 120 feet being the shortest allowable size.

Care of the Rope

As with any piece of fine equipment, careful use and appropriate care in storage will assure longer use. Rope should be coiled loosely and stored in a cool, clean place out of direct sunlight. Stepping on the rope or pulling it unprotected over rough surfaces or sharp rocks permits accelerated wear, and in time tiny rock particles will work their way between, and eventually cut, the fibers.

Periodic machine washing (Delicate Fabrics setting) with mild soap, and drip drying will help prolong the rope's life. Never let harmful chemicals, like battery acid, sun creams, and insect repellents, come into contact with the rope.

Headwear

A well-constructed hard hat for climbing will prevent injury from rocks and pitons falling from above and

Helmets should be worn by climbers to protect against head injuries. This Joe Brown model, which passes all UIAA tests, has a laminated fiberglass shell with urethane foam liner. Of course, a chin strap is essential. Note the visorless design, allowing excellent visibility in all directions while still providing adequate skull protection. *(Alan Bagg)*

avoid head-to-rock contact in the event of a fall. While many Midwest climbers neglect to wear one, a helmet should be worn at all times on the rope, and even off the rope, whenever there is a chance of loose rock being kicked down from above.

Helmets, to provide adequate protection, must shield the head without restricting peripheral vision. Therefore, they must not be too long around the ears, or slip down over the forehead, or have too large a visor. The hat must have an adjustable inside shock-absorbing harness that prevents the outside shell from touching the head; the hat will absorb the blow without transferring it to the skull. A chin strap keeps the hat securely in place, even when struck by hard objects such as rocks.

Proper fit is an important consideration. Most hard hats made specifically for climbing have an adjustable interior headband so that fine adjustments can be made for a perfect fit. Better quality hats will be UIAA approved.

Hardware

A protection system is necessary when rapelling and aid climbing, and at some places along many of the free-climbing routes. Protection consists of a means of anchoring your body to the rock.

Protection was previously made by passing the climbing rope through carabiners attached to hardened steel spikes called pitons, hammered into the rock for maximum protection (when piton placement was properly carried out). But, as I have mentioned, piton craft is banned in areas of the Midwest where its heavy traffic would quickly disintegrate the route. Climbers now rely almost solely on artificial (usually aluminum alloy) chockstones, referred to as "chocks" or "nuts," for their hardware protection.

CHOCKS

The greatest advantage of chocks is that as quickly removable points of protection they do not damage the rock. Incorporating great strength with light weight (they are manufactured from stainless steel or aluminum alloy), these devices are normally placed in cracks with only the aid of fingers, but are sometimes hammered into tough placements. Unlike pitons that can pull out in a sharp fall, chocks wedge themselves deeper into the crack upon absorbing the shock of the fall. Chocks are threaded with slings of nylon webbing, perlon rope, or wire cable and attached to the climbing rope by a runner and carabiner.

British climbers reportedly invented and first used chocks, which stemmed from their method of using natural chockstones and runners as a means of protection. Before today's sophisticated chocks, climbers used regular machine nuts with slings through the holes.

Chocks are faster to place and remove, yield a more aesthetically "pure" and quiet sense of climbing ("at one with the rock, not violating it"), and for the most part are a surer means of protection. Chocks are notably superior in loose rock or expanding flakes.

Since they can be "jammed" into cracks that are narrower at the bottom, wedge-shaped "stopper" chocks are slid into cracks until they are tightly snugged. Stopper chocks are easily used by many climbers since their consistent edge-like taper resembles the average taper of constrictions within cracks and therefore allows a large area of chock surface to be in contact with the rock. Stoppers are made in a planned progression of sizes to fit cracks ranging from about ⅛ to 1¼ inches in width. Some companies make numbered "half stoppers" which fit halfway between adjacent sizes of the original series, allowing almost a perfect fit.

Chocks are available with either wire or perlon slings. Wire has the advantages of being stronger in the smaller sizes, completely waterproof, and longer lasting than perlon. Perlon is superior in its choice of line length and color for coding.

Eccentrically shaped chocks can be "cammed" as well as jammed. If one is placed in a crack, under a load it will roll over and wedge itself sideways in the crack and prevent pulling out. Kirk's Kamms is one of these true-cam chocks and is available from Colorado Mountain Industries.

Six-sided eccentric nuts, commonly called hex or hexcentric nuts, allow offset placements and have the advantage of one hex fitting different size cracks if cocked right or left. They are available from a number of outfitters and are more expensive than stopper chocks.

A fourth and very recent development in chock design is a camming chock called a "cog." Cogs are a type of hex nut with rounded corners and concave faces that have even better cam action than hex nuts. With this unique shape, cogs allow a greater variety of placement opportunities, such as in old piton scars, cracks with frayed edges, and even in solution pockets whose restricted edges normally prevent the entrance of conventional hexes. Manufactured by Clogwyn from aluminum alloy, cogs can be stacked to bridge large cracks because of the meshing of concave and convex surfaces.

The fifth type of chock consists of various size lengths of tubular aluminum which are placed endwise in cracks. These tube chocks are lighter and more easily carried than the same number of conventional chocks or nuts and offer better protection for wide jam cracks. They are available from the Great Pacific Iron Works.

There are also I-beam "Beamchocks" from CMI and

Wedge-shaped stopper chocks resemble the average taper of cracks and allow a large area of contact with the rock. They are available in a graduated series of sizes. *(Forrest Mountaineering)*

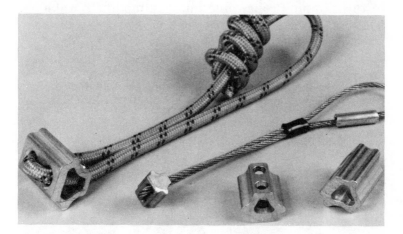

A recent development in chock design is a camming chock called a "cog," a type of hex nut with rounded corners and concave faces. They "cam" more easily than conventional hexes. *(Alan Bagg)*

Tube chocks are lighter and more easily carried than the same number of conventional chocks or nuts and offer better protection for wide jam cracks. *(Great Pacific Iron Works)*

"Titons," a T-beam chock that comes in very handy for spanning cracks too wide for a conventional chock to fit in. Titons are available from Forrest Mountaineering, Ltd.

CARABINERS

Carabiners, strong metal snap links similar to safety pins, are used to connect a variety of elements in the climbing chain. Normally made of aluminum alloy in oval or somewhat pear-shaped configurations about four inches long, carabiners connect slings or runners to the climbing rope, function as a modified brake bar used for rappelling, connect belayers to rocks or trees, and turn a sling into a seat harness in seconds. They can also be used to carry hardware. Carabiners have

Carabiners are strong aluminum-alloy snap links, similiar to safety pins, used to connect a variety of elements in the climbing chain. *(Forrest Mountaineering)*

either a locking or nonlocking spring gate that should open easily under a load.

One of the most popular carabiners sold in the United States is the Chouinard modified-D shape which is very strong; it is capable of holding a long fall even with the gate open. They are more expensive than standard other carabiners and are less suited to carry equipment, so some climbers often carry both kinds. Another advantage of the Chouinard carabiner is that a slight bulge near the gate lets you feel on which side the gate opens (a big plus on desperate 5.10s).

Important points to check when buying new carabiners are spring action of the gate (should be smooth but not too strong), that the gate action mates properly, that there are no metal burrs, and that the carabiner tests to a minimum of 2,500 pounds with the gate closed. Gate rivets should be tightly press fitted and peened over for extra strength when the gate is under a side load, such as when used as a carabiner brake. The Chouinard carabiner even has a gate latch opening which is shaped so that the gate locks shut under a load of more than two hundred pounds.

A carabiner should never be oiled since dirt will cling to it and clog the gate.

Software

RUNNERS OR SLINGS

Runners are general-purpose slings made of tubular or flat webbing, knotted with a water knot or sewn together to form a loop for carrying equipment. Typically, a single runner is four or five feet long, and a double, eight or ten feet. Runners are most commonly used to reduce the rope drag produced when placing out-of-the-way protection. Normally a dozen should handle most pitches in the Midwest, but since the runners are placed over rock horns, around trees, and on literally everything else in sight, as well as with chocks to provide points of security, a dozen may not be enough.

Longer runners can be fashioned from about a ten-foot sling, which can be used as a "diaper" sling on rappels. Therefore, a variety of material and lengths of runners should be carried, looped over the shoulder and under the opposite arm, or in a rucksack.

Flat webbing from a half through one-inch widths and a good selection of rope diameters (9 mm. probably is standard) fit a variety of situations.

Only those runners that are tied with knots (as opposed to sewn slings for hardware) should be trusted as part of a protection system. All perlon and nylon sling materials, when cut, should have the ends immediately fused by holding a match or other flame to it to prevent ravelling.

In my opinion rope makes the best material for chock slings, and the webbing is best suited for "swami belts" or rappel slings, attaching rope or wire chock runners to the climbing rope, equipment slings, and making an etrier used in aid climbing. A note on attaching runners to wired chocks: at no time should a runner be tied directly to the wire loop. Instead, use a carabiner to connect the wire and runner because under the tension of a fall, the nylon sling can be cut by the small-diameter wire.

As a general rule, chocks which do not allow use of perlon in diameters of 5 mm. or larger should be wired.

Etriers

Etriers are short rope ladders used in direct aid climbing. Stiffer nontubular webbing works best in keeping the shape of the "steps" formed in the rope. The webbing etrier should be designed to suit the individual's size and type of climbing. A few points to consider in their construction are mentioned here.

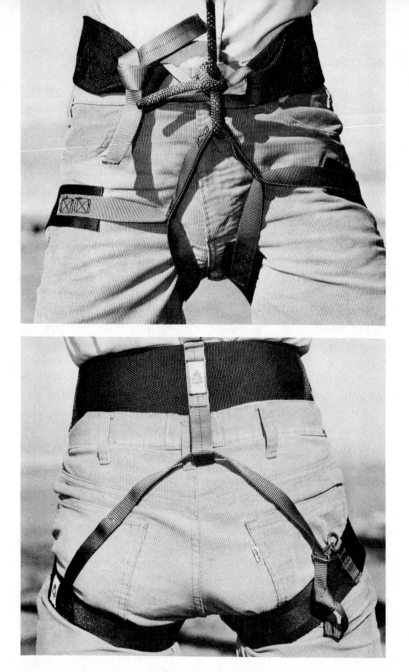

The Forrest climbing harness provides a secure and comfortable seat for rappels and hanging belays, as well as for free and aid climbing. It is designed to distribute impact force to the thighs as well as the waist in the event of a fall. *(Forrest Mountaineering)*

In order to be of greatest utility, the top loop of the etrier should be positioned to provide the highest level step possible while maintaining the free carabiner barely within reach for use as a handhold. Meeting this condition will allow the top loop to be used more than 95 percent of the time. On low-angle faces, the maximum reach is obtained by using a Hero Loop (see Glossary) clipped into the etrier carabiner.

Today, as more climbs are being pushed free and artificial pitches are being followed on Jumars, extra consideration should be given to the ease of carrying the etrier. A shorter etrier carries easily over the shoulder. An etrier with two large loops deploys quickly when the top loop is placed around the neck.

To construct the webbing etrier, cut the proper length of webbing. One-inch flat or tubular webbing is normally used, but for special purposes where weight is of primary importance, half or three-quarter inch may be used. About thirteen feet are required for the standard three-loop etrier. A length of ten feet, ten inches, makes a good two-loop etrier.

Form a large loop with a nine-inch overlap and tie the Frost knot—a simple overhand knot over the triple-thickness section—to fashion the carabiner loop. Form individual loops with overhand knots leaving about four inches of eccentricity in the loops. While tightening the knots, first carefully by hand, then by vigorous bounding in every loop, maintain a close check to insure that the etrier dimensions, particularly loop eccentricity, are maintained.

Clothing and Packs

Gloves

Gloves are very helpful to the beginning and intermediate climber. They not only save the hands for delicate climbing later, but bolster one's courage and margin of safety for rappelling and belaying. It only makes sense to wear them.

I prefer a snug-fitting, medium-thick pair of leather gloves, thin enough to allow the feel of the rope passing through the hands but thick enough to prevent a severe rope burn, even if the rope gets away momentarily and races through the belayer's hands. Of course, a good grip even when wet is all important. Leather gloves can be treated with neat's-foot oil to keep them soft and supple for years. A good glove for climbers is a goatskin type sold by various climbing outfitters. Another type, sold in most hardware stores, is the typical "cowboy" or wrangler glove made of calfskin.

Gloves can also be used to protect the shoulder when no rappel pad is available.

RUCKSACK DAY PACK

A well-designed day pack in which each climber can carry personal gear, such as cameras, chocks and ropes, slings, perhaps lunch, and miscellaneous paraphernalia, is a welcome addition to the climber's standard gear.

As an optional item, the rucksack comes in very handy. A good one has ample space for the day's outing, without a frame, and preferably features a leather, reinforced canvas, or nylon bottom for longer wear (especially when plopped down on rocks).

As with anything else, the more money spent on a pack, the better the quality you can expect. Many distributors offer the teardrop-type day pack or some modification of it. While size is a matter of opinion, I believe that a rucksack should contain at least a thousand cubic inches of cargo area and a divider, so two compartments are available. This keeps gear segregated and is much handier during a hurried search. Instead of rummaging through everything, it will be

A well-designed day pack, like this Camp Trails divided teardrop, allows each climber to carry personal gear, such as cameras, chocks, ropes, slings, lunch, and other climbing paraphernalia. *(Alan Bagg)*

easier to find the sought-after article if the pack has some semblance of order.

It should also have reinforced seams and strong nylon zippers, and be made of a heavy-duty nylon cloth like Cordura or some other very strong material. Better packs also have leather attachment points for lashing on extra gear, like climbing ropes, ice axes, and crampons. Climbers can expect to pay $20 to $40 for a superior rucksack.

RAIN GEAR

The best rain gear I have found for climbing (and for just about any other outdoor activity) is the three-

A large day pack like this Hine Snowbridge Cirque II allows enough gear to be carried on miniexpeditions. *(Hine-Snowbridge)*

quarter (or calf length) *cagoule,* named after the French word meaning monk's cloak.

The *cagoule* has several advantages over a common poncho, since it has sleeves instead of just armholes, for ease of movement, and complete waterproof capabilities. It also contains an outside pocket for essential items like map and compass.

A hooded *cagoule* can also be turned into a survival tent by covering your feet with a packsack and drawing the bottom drawstring tight. This way you can sleep through the bad weather if caught without a way to get out of the rain. Able to be compressed to just a handful of material, the *cagoule* fits neatly into the rucksack and can be carried anywhere.

Better workmanship means waterproof seams, elasticized storm cuffs, a full-length zippered front with storm flap, and drawstrings at the neck and feet. A good *cagoule* costs between $25 and $40, depending on the manufacturer.

part 2

3

Climbing

Climbing Areas: Illinois (12 areas)

Shawnee National Forest Section (8 areas)
   Giant City State Park (2 areas)
   1. Makanda Bluffs
   2. Devil's Standtable
   Drapers Bluff
   Cedar Bluffs
   Ferne Clyffe State Park
   Stone Face One
   Stone Face Two
   Dixon Springs State Park
   Mississippi Palisades State Park (4 areas)
   1. Twin Sisters
   2. Open Bible
   3. Sentinel Area (West Face)
   4. Sentinel Quadrangle (East Face)

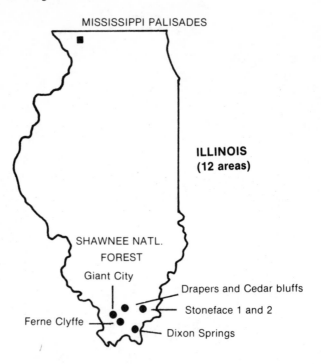

Rock-climbing areas in Illinois are found at the extreme north and south ends of the state, with not much else in between. In the northwestern corner lies Mississippi Palisades State Park, near Savanna, in Carroll County. Here steep limestone bluffs along the Mississippi River give rise to the park's name and to excellent climbing for chimney (see Glossary) buffs. The Mississippi Palisades, a popular place often used as a training ground to perfect climbing skills, is already known to many climbers throughout the Midwest.

The climbing found in the southern end of the state, much of it in the Shawnee National Forest, near Carbondale, is not as well known and offers explorers a good chance to put up their own routes, possibly over rock that has never been traversed before. Here, a concentration of Illinois state parks dotting the immense Shawnee National Forest comprises a number of major climbing sites, with plenty of acres left over for some minor and undiscovered ones.

Illinois has hundreds of rock outcrops, many of which are located in its southern tip. A United States Forest Service map of the Shawnee National Forest, which covers a large part of this area, illustrates why this geological playground is a climber's Mecca.

Almost all of the points of interest listed on the national forest map (some two or three dozen) are climbing areas on which climbers have put up routes. The hard sandstone outcroppings make for an infinite number of climb routes, much like the crag climbing in England. These thirty- to two-hundred-foot high escarpments seem to have been sprinkled throughout the forest in such numbers that most have routes that have never been named. Climbers who live in the southern Illinois area know of them, and "via the grapvine" is the way to find out about them. Climbers interested in discovering new areas that are not specifically named in this book can get in touch with Bob Marsh at the Chockstone Mountaineering Shop in Carbondale.

Topographic maps of this part of the state also are very helpful to climbers, since a skillful reader of a topo quad can pick out potential bluffs and outcrops depicted on the map, then explore them leisurely. Marsh claims southern Illinois climbers have a unique situation because of the variety of available climbing areas there. The climbs in southern Illinois are short and hard, on fair to good sandstone, and rarely are more than a hundred feet in height. Concentrated around six different bluff systems, many are described in more detail under each climbing section that follows.

The intricacies of sandstone climbing will come slowly to the granite-hard climber, but the sandstone addicts swear there is no climbing like it. Don't look for clear soaring handcracks or nice square handholds here. Instead, bottoming cracks and solution pockets, with a sprinkling of delicate friction, are the typical terrain features on sandstone. The newcomer will find protection to be more psychological than on harder rock because here the chock bites the rock instead of vice versa. Sandstone creates imaginative leaders because protection is much harder to find as well.

A climbing guide that details particular routes in all six of the major climbing areas in southern Illinois is *The Gritstone Mountaineer,* by Adam Grosowsky, which is sold by mail order through Chockstone Mountaineering, University and Walnut streets, Carbondale, Illinois 62901; or Pine Mountain Wilderness Equipment, 1529 South Greenriver Road, Evansville, Indiana 47715. The cost is approximately $6, postage paid.

Giant City State Park

DESCRIPTION

Giant City State Park has parts of its 3,664 acres in both Jackson and Union counties. Near Makanda, Illinois, the park is part of the Shawnee National Forest and lies within the Shawnee Hills, which vary in elevation from 500 to 1,060 feet. A group of huge sandstone blocks, to which the name "Giant City" has been applied, gives the park its name. The park is situated in a belt of hills that cross the narrow part of southern Illinois, which ages ago was a lowland plain that slowly emerged from the sea.

As the region gradually rose, the stream which flowed over it carved out deeper and deeper valleys. Now only isolated ridges and knobs remain. The hard and resistant rocks stand as steep walls along the valleys; soft rocks have been worn down to gentle

Sheer walls offer numerous climbing opportunities at Giant City State Park, near Makanda. *(Illinois Dept. of Conservation)*

slopes. All of this produces an area suggestive of ancient worn mountains, with some of the most striking examples of stream erosion in hard rock.

Located just outside the glaciated area of Illinois, the park was perhaps affected by the proximity of the glacier and its melting waters, but the only visible effect is the soil (called loess), which is rock "flour" produced by the grinding action of the glacier and deposited by the wind everywhere on the uplands.

The bedrock belongs to the Pennsylvania age. It is generally exposed or thinly covered along the walls and in the side gullies of the streams and is known as "coal measures" because all of the coal beds in the Central and Appalachian states occur in the system.

The rock attracting the most attention is a massive sandstone formation that composes the upper part of the hills and forms precipitous bluffs wherever conditions are favorable. The huge blocks of rock that form the Giant City section are masses of this sandstone which separated from the adjacent parent ledge, much like the appearance of granite flakes but in much greater proportions. This separation occurred as streams cut through the massive sandstone into softer rock, such as shale, and the soft rock was removed faster than the hard, gradually undercutting the hard rock until eventually masses were broken off.

As a result of the numerous up-and-down movements of the surface of the earth in southern Illinois, the harder rocks have been cracked or joined in many directions. The sandstone at Giant City is jointed along two general directions and the resulting blocks settle down readily wherever the support provided by the shale below is reduced. Since shale is soft and slippery when wet, the joint blocks gradually slide down the shale slopes and thus move away from the parent ledge. One of the most interesting natural rock formations from this process is the Devil's Standtable, just west of the park's interpretive center.

Where exposed to weathering, the sandstone has been stained by minerals carried by water seepage in various shades of red, brown, and yellow, while the unweathered stone shows white or a light buff color.

The whole southern Illinois area is a paradise for the outdoor lover. A large part of this end of the state forms the Shawnee National Forest with its overlapping of northern and southern species of plant and animal life. There are more than eight hundred different ferns and flowering plants in the park, and in the spring the woods are tinted with redbud, wahoo, and flowering dogwood. Red cedar and southern yellow pine are well represented in the more than seventy-five different trees found in the park. Huge peach and apple orchards, visible from the park area, are exquisite when in bloom. May is the peak flowering month when about a hundred seventy different types may be found.

**Map showing loca-
tion of Giant City State Park**

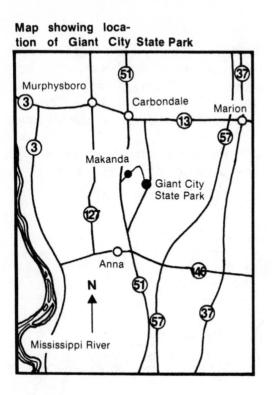

LOCATION

Giant City State Park is located twelve miles south of Carbondale, off U.S. Route 51. The four park entrances are well marked by·numerous highway signs.

The Makanda (Illinois) USGS 7½′ quad covers Giant City State Park. The Makanda Bluffs, near the main park entrance on the northeast end, and the Devil's Standtable, reached by taking the blacktop road northwest into the park's interior, are the only two areas where park officials allow climbing. Other guidebooks have listed more areas, but these have been closed because park officials fear that climbers would damage the somewhat fragile rock and plant systems in the park.

Climbing

Giant City State Park is considered Mecca for southern Illinois climbing. It is a very popular area and has an almost "circus atmosphere" during summer weekends. The popularity of the park and its easy access to climb sites in part account for the area's intensive use by climbers.

Makanda Bluffs is the main attraction, containing the most concentrated selection of routes, but the Devil's Standtable is also climbable.

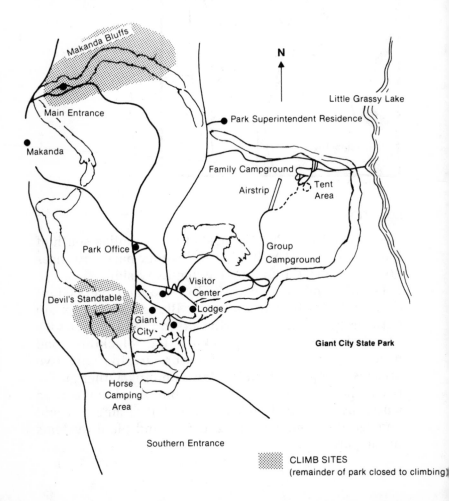

Giant City State Park

CLIMB SITES
(remainder of park closed to climbing)

This area is typical of the southern Illinois sandstone climbing mentioned earlier. Forty- to ninety-foot cliffs composed of rounded sandstone, riddled with solution pockets and bottoming cracks, abound in this park. Climbing techniques needed for this type of rock are delicate friction, ingenious route finding, and picking your way from pocket to fissure to shallow crack, instead of following a granite crack for a hundred feet.

The routes vary considerably in difficulty, ranging from 5.0 to 5.11, so any climber can find something to his or her liking. Since cracks are often rounded and shallow, it is difficult to find protection, although patient and daring climbers can find leadable climbs. For the most part, however, the climbs are top roped.

Makanda Bluffs

The Makanda Bluffs, not specifically shown as such on the state park maps, are the highest, cleanest, and most crowded cliffs in the park. There are a lot of 5.6+ and a fair number of 5.10 climbs among the slabs, cracks, traverses, chimneys, and overhanging dihedral and layback sections that are all part of the makeup of the rocks here.

Dead Dog, Names Unknown, Dihedral, No Name, and Electric Kool-Aid Acid Trip are all 5.10 or harder climbs. There is a good blend of easier climbs, too. At one time, climbing was allowed on the Streets section of Giant City Park. This area is now closed to all roped climbing.

The bluffs are covered with gray-green lichens, mosses, ferns, and herbacious plants. Alum root and wild hydrangea are common flowering plants on the bluff surface, and park officials are afraid this delicate ecosystem is in danger of being ruined.

The massive hill of sandstone rests on a layer of shale, but earth movements and freezing cracks have created fissures on the edges of the main stone block. Erosion has undercut the outer edges of cracked pieces, and they are slowly sliding away from the main body of rock. As the fissures widen, they become these rock canyons known as "streets," with the "buildings" lining the canyon valleys.

Devil's Standtable

The chain of bluffs of which the Devil's Standtable is a part has some reasonably good climbs, and climbing is allowed here. There are usually fewer people climbing here than at Makanda Bluffs, because it is a smaller area with less variety of rock.

The Devil's Standtable has at least two good climbs. One is on the west face, called Chris's Climb, and the other is a nameless one on the north face. Leading here would be folly, for there is no place for protection. Both are slightly overhung and are rated 5.6.

Nothing can be done safely under the overhang, except for a climb that is reached by traversing out from the landing that is used to start the west face of the Standtable. Traverse to the left about fifteen feet, then up the obvious crack. As far as I know, the climb has never been executed, possibly because it is often wet. There is also a host of small climbs far down to the left.

This free-standing pillar of rock is the product of the selective erosion of the sandstone bluff and slippage on the underlying eroded shale. Like the formation of the streets of Giant City, this pillar was once a part of the bluff that cracked loose. It has slowly slid downhill from the bluff as the underlying shale eroded, and the gradual erosion of its surface has created its present shape as a giant sandstone mushroom. To those who named it, it must have seemed like the kind of place from which a devil would preach.

The immense shelter cave leading up to the Standtable was heavily used by Indians during the Late Woodland period. Most of the artifacts and burials were removed from the cave before laws provided protection of such cultural resources.

The honeycombed areas of sandstone on the bluff surface are of great interest to geology students. These bluffs were formed as part of a great river-delta area during the "coal ages" of Illinois. Sometime between their formation and the present, ground water with dissolved iron compounds seeped into the sandstone. The iron precipitated into hematite (iron ore) deposits within the softer sandstone. The wind and water erosion of the bluff surface has left the harder iron deposits standing out in relief. In some places, these form the pockmarked "honeycombs" and in others they appear as thick, dark ridges that form ornate patterns. The soil below the bluff is permeated with the eroded sand crystals, giving the ground a sparkling appearance in direct sunlight.

ACCOMMODATIONS AND OTHER ATTRACTIONS

There are 120 camp sites among 4 campgrounds located within the park boundaries and a good number of private camp grounds near Carbondale and Makanda. These two towns also offer a fair range of motel accommodations.

A large family camp ground, with a separate section for tents, is located on the east side of the park for those who prefer a more primitive camping experience. A class "C" camp ground is used for youth camping and two class "A" camp grounds, complete with electricity, sanitary station, and utility building including showers and flush toilets for tent and trailer users, also are available.

Camping fees are charged depending on the quality

of the camp sites, "A" having the highest degree of development. Camping permits must be secured from the park manager.

At the southernmost tip of Giant City State Park, the state-operated lodge has a lounge, large dining room, banquet halls, and snack bar. There are a dozen rental cabins nearby, a blend of modern and rustic, available by reservation only. The lodge and cabins are open from March until November, but the rest of the park is open year round, except on Christmas and New Year's Day or when weather conditions necessitate the closing of road.

For more details about Giant City State Park, write or call the Site Superintendent, RR 1, Makanda, IL 62958, (618) 457-4836.

Private camp grounds in the Carbondale area include Crab Orchard Lake Campgrounds on State Highway 13 with 310 sites, many of them with utilities, and Devil's Kitchen Lake Campground, 9 miles southeast on Lake Road, with 38 sites. Ferne Clyffe State Park, near Goreville, is another public camp ground that has 50 sites and a few climbing areas of its own (See Ferne Clyffe listing).

Drapers Bluff Area

DESCRIPTION

Drapers Bluff is one of the finest areas for climbing in southern Illinois because of its abundance of good rock, with the highest average route height in the area. For the most part, the secluded bluffs soar 120 feet high and offer fantastic views of the surrounding Union County countryside.

The bluff's overhang features, that run the entire length of the cliffs for about two miles, are the main feature of this area and offer sufficient problems to make them a good challenge for intermediate to advanced climbers. Many of the routes are two-pitch climbs because of the superior height of the bluffs.

Location

Drapers Bluff is located on the Lick Creek (Illinois) 7½' USGS quadrangle. The state highway maps don't show the area very well, but they will get you into the general vicinity if you follow Interstate 57 south from Marion about ten miles to the Lick Creek exit. A Shawnee National Forest map lists Drapers right on the Union-Johnson county line, about one and a half miles east of Lick Creek. A rural forest road runs east from Lick Creek, and the bluffs will appear on your left a couple of miles east of town. Continue past the bluffs until you see a turnoff for a church; its parking lot is a good place to leave your car.

To reach the climb sites, walk a hundred yards back down the road (in the direction from which you arrived) and cross the field to the front of the bluffs. From here head into the trees and diagonally traverse to the start of the rock. This seemingly cumbersome approach avoids private property.

Climbing

Drapers Bluff features a troublesome overhang area that runs the entire two-mile length of the bluff, about seventy-five feet above the ground. At most points, a ledge runs beneath the overhang from which the first pitch ends and the second pitch starts toward the longer routes. There are climbs all along the bluff area and Grosowsky's guide describes most of these in detail, including starting points and what to expect.

The Overhang, a 5.8 route, is the first climb to locate on the first large (about twenty-five foot) outcropping.

It begins at a thin crack that runs up the fifteen-foot face, at the start of the rock (just past the trees from the church parking lot).

From the overhang you can continue along the bluffs until you come to a large, boulder-strewn gully, which is the only descent route for about a mile. A buttress-like formation which sits just to the left of the gully has a nice jam crack to climb. There is also a chimney where the buttress meets the face.

About fifty yards farther, there is a chimney where the ledge ends. About twenty-five feet left of the big chimney break is a series of cracks and chimneys that run diagonally (slightly right) up the wall. These are fun to scramble.

There is an absence of routes for about the next hundred yards, but if you continue on to where the bluffs start getting higher, there are more climbs that start at the base of the bluffs (across from the barbed-wire fence). By proceeding forty feet farther you will come to a very vertical blank face capped by tiers of overhang. Some aid pitches are found here on the Bookshelf Blues and Thrutch routes.

There aren't any climbing routes for a long distance after this. Follow the path for about one hundred fifty yards, until you come to a walk-up chimney that takes you to a big ledge under the huge overhang. (This is the ledge and overhang section of the bluff.) The ledge is about fifteen feet wide for about a hundred yards, with the ground about fifty feet below and the top blocked by the overhang. All climbs here end on this ledge. Bad Day, an F7 climb, marks the end of the overhang and ledge section. The bluffs open up again from here.

There are still numerous routes—some difficult due to aid pitches, and some easier—all the way down the bluffs. Many have been climbed but not named or described, and a good number are still waiting to be climbed, offering the route finder an exciting challenge.

ACCOMMODATIONS AND OTHER ATTRACTIONS

Ferne Clyffe State Park, in nearby Goreville, offers fifty sites for camping, for both tents and trailers. All campers must obtain a permit from the park superintendent before entering the camp ground.

Cedar Lake Ranch, about ten miles northeast of Vienna, has seventy-five sites with electricity, water, showers, and other facilities. This is a privately owned commercial camp ground.

Marion offers a number of motels to the north of Drapers Bluff.

Cedar Bluffs

DESCRIPTION

Cedar Bluffs is essentially a continuation of Drapers Bluff and is sometimes referred to as the "backside of Drapers." But on topographic maps, Cedar Bluffs exists in its own right. The bluffs are very similar to Drapers in every respect, except they are shorter in length and height. Cedar also has the added attraction of a shorter approach and a greater density of routes in a smaller area.

LOCATION

To get to Cedar Bluffs, follow the Drapers description to the church. A path leads up the hill on the bell side of the church. Go up the path and turn left at the top. This trail continues to the bottom of the bluffs where the climbs begin, by a huge overhang which forms a cave.

CLIMBING

There are still many routes to establish on Cedar Bluffs. Grosowsky describes a good number in his booklet (a must for the area), but he is one of the few persons that have documented the climbs here.

The climbing here is an explorer's delight—so much is new and undiscovered. The bluffs extend a great distance and there are numerous routes to the left of the cave at the starting point. A large amphitheater-like section of the bluffs contains a nice ledge about halfway up.

This area is for exploring.

ACCOMMODATIONS AND OTHER ATTRACTIONS

See Drapers Bluff.

Ferne Clyffe State Park

DESCRIPTION

This 1,073-acre state park in Johnson County can boast of the most beautiful natural sights in this part of the state. The park is in a scenic area of valleys, dells, canyons, and brooks. Ferne Clyffe is close to the Drapers and Cedar bluffs area, so it might be nice to combine the trips into a long weekend.

Ferne Clyffe State Park has a central valley from which radiates a number of gorges and canyons containing shady dells, natural cathedrals, domes, brooks, cascades, and rills. Several so-called caves are not truly caves, but great protruding ledges of rock that make an arched roof.

Hawk's Cave is a sheer cliff of stone; so hewn by wind and water that an excavation has been made at its base at least a hundred fifty feet long and as many feet tall. The cave has a natural pulpit and excellent acoustics.

In the fall the beauty is enhanced by the colors of gum, maple, dogwood, and sumac trees, which combine with the more somber shades of the oak, ash, and other hardwoods.

Ferne Clyffe State Park in Johnson County offers great climbing possibilities not far from Drapers Bluffs. *(Illinois Dept. of Conservation)*

In 1960, a sixteen-acre fishing lake was built near the northeastern foot of Round Bluff. The maximum depth of the lake is twenty-one feet and the shoreline is about one mile around. Boats are not permitted but fishing from the banks is popular. There are several picnic areas throughout the valley and near the lake, with tables, park stoves, toilets, and drinking water. There are five hiking trails that wind throughout the park for about seven miles.

LOCATION

Ferne Clyffe Park is located one mile southwest of Goreville on SH 37, about twelve miles south of Marion, in Johnson County. State and county maps and the Shawnee National Forest map show the location well (or see the attached map).

Round Bluff, the main climbing area at the southern end of the park, is accessible by road, then across a small stream. Park in the large lot provided.

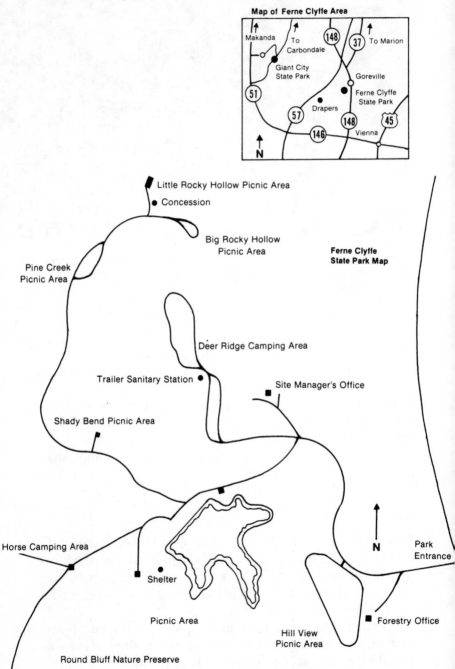

Map of Ferne Clyffe Area

Makanda
To Carbondale
148
37
To Marion

Giant City State Park

Goreville

51

Drapers

Ferne Clyffe State Park

57

148

146

45

Vienna

N

Little Rocky Hollow Picnic Area
● Concession

Big Rocky Hollow Picnic Area

Ferne Clyffe State Park Map

Pine Creek Picnic Area

Deer Ridge Camping Area

Trailer Sanitary Station ●

Site Manager's Office ■

Shady Bend Picnic Area

Horse Camping Area ■

■ Shelter ●

N

Park Entrance

Picnic Area

Hill View Picnic Area

■ Forestry Office

Round Bluff Nature Preserve

The USGS quad that encompasses Ferne Clyffe State Park is the Goreville (Illinois) 7½′ quadrangle. Since the park is located so close to the edge of that map, you might also choose to order the adjacent (west) Lick Creek 7½′ quad (also useful for locating climbs at Drapers Bluff).

CLIMBING

Ferne Clyffe's Round Bluff is a large outcrop of very compact sandstone with an overhanging base, similar to Makanda Bluff at Giant City State Park. There are not nearly as many routes here as at Makanda, but they are all high-quality climbs.

Known by the names Rusty Pin, Missouri Breaks, Hawk's Beak, and Under the Influence, the routes are quite difficult; all are rated at least F7. Rusty Pin contains an A1 aid section which can also be done free (rated at 5.10 if done free) over the overhang at the bottom.

A difficult overhang called Fiddler on the Roof (5.11).
(Adam Grosowsky)

ACCOMMODATIONS AND OTHER ATTRACTIONS

About fifty sites are available for camping in the Deer Ridge camp ground in the center of the park, both for tents and trailers. Electricity, a sanitary disposal station, and shower building are also available. A separate camp ground for horses and their riders is located at the southern end of the park.

The same accommodations listed under Giant City and Drapers Bluff also apply here. (See the area map for approximate locations of these other climb sites.)

For more details about the Ferne Clyffe Park, write or call the Park Manager, Box 125, Goreville, IL 62939, (618) 995-2411.

Stone Faces One and Two

DESCRIPTION

Stone Face is the hottest new climbing area in southern Illinois. There are two sets of bluffs in the Stone Face area which constitute two different climbing areas: Stone Face One, an easily accessible set of bluffs that rarely exceeds forty feet in height, and Stone Face Two, a great bluff climbing area with probably the nicest bluffs in southern Illinois but containing no trails. Therefore, a long bushwhack is required to get to Stone Face Two.

Both areas offer some of the finest climbing southern Illinois has to offer.

LOCATION

Stone Faces One and Two are located in Saline County, about six miles southeast of Harrisburg (twelve miles by road), near the town of Rudement, in the Shawnee National Forest. USGS quads Rudement (Illinois) 7½′ and Equality (Illinois) 15′ cover this area. Stone Face is marked on the national forest map.

To get to Stone Face, take SH 13 east from Harrisburg about six miles and turn south (right) on the county road that leads to Rudement. Drive until you see the sign on the side of the road (about six more miles), then follow a maze of roads to the parking area to the bluffs of Stone Face One. From here, take the Stone Face lower-view trail to the base of the bluffs and turn right.

To reach Stone Face Two, turn right when coming out of the parking area. Drive for two miles to a jeep road heading up towards the bluffs. Go up the jeep road as far as you can and bushwhack to the cliffs. Locating a seventy-five foot slice in the rock will put you in the right vicinity of a number of excellent climbs.

CLIMBING

STONE FACE ONE

Many climbs exist here, some charted routes (by Adam Grosowsky) and others left to the imagination of innovative climbers. Midnight Cowboy, an F9+ climb, consists of a top-roped pitch around a small tower, leaning against the bluff which forms a needle's eye. An F7 climb called Graduation is a landmark on the right side of the tower. Look for a zigzagging crack and you'll find many climbs in this area. The next fifty yards are littered with routes in the 5.3 to 5.6 range.

There is also a boxed-in amphitheater area with a chimney crack (5.7) in a back corner. Imagination is the only limit to the number of routes in this area.

STONE FACE TWO

The climbs here are all F7 or harder. Grosowsky's *Gritstone Mountaineer* booklet can be consulted for a fairly comprehensive description of eight known

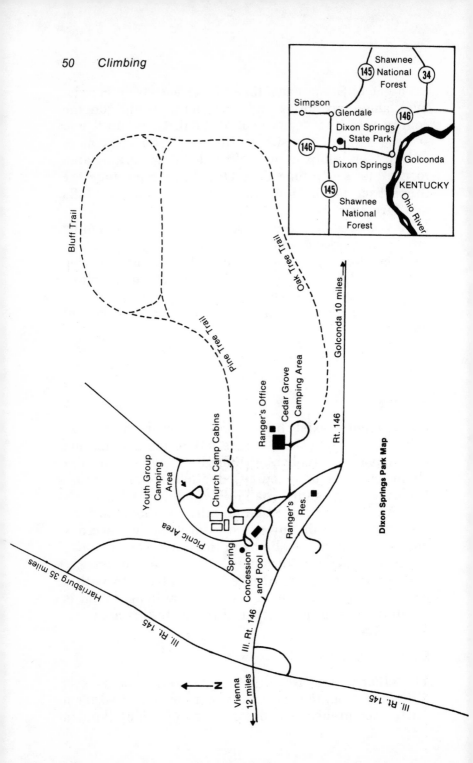

Dixon Springs Park Map

routes in this area. There are many more to explore and discover on your own.

ACCOMMODATIONS AND OTHER ATTRACTIONS

Stone Face is close enough to Harrisburg that motels are normally not a problem. Camping facilities in the national forest are excellent, with four forest service camp grounds and one county camp ground within ten miles over the forest road to the east. All the camp grounds can be located easily on the forest service map, including Garden of the Gods Recreation Area, Karbers Ridge, Camp Cadiz, Pounds Hollow Recreation Area, and the Saline County Conservation Area.

Private camp grounds are also available. The Redbud-Bellsmith Campground on Forest Road (FR) 848 offers 22 sites in a rustic setting. Dogwood Hollow Campground, a half mile east on FR 17 between SH 34 and SH 1 offers 70 sites in a rustic, semi-wooded area.

Dixon Springs State Park

DESCRIPTION

Dixon Springs State Park in the Shawnee National Forest is one of three state parks in the Illinois extension of the Ozark Mountains. The park is on a giant block of rock which dropped two hundred feet along a fault line that extends northwest across Pope County.

The entire county is hilly; during rainy weather rivulets everywhere cascade down the hills in the park area, forming more than fifteen hundred waterfalls of varying sizes and heights.

Rapid erosion has exposed the rock in various forms, and large blocks appear as though they had burst from the ground. In places, the rock has broken or slumped away to produce the effect of canyons.

Bold cliffs and beetling crags overhang a brook

below; gigantic boulders overgrown with ferns, ivy, lichens, and moss fringe the hillside. Squirrels romp among the branches in beech groves and stands of fragrant cedars and massive oaks. Giant, century-old trees interlock above the small creek as cliffs rise on either side. Huge boulders are scattered throughout the valley.

Equally intriguing are the names given numerous points of interest, including Album Rock, Red Man's Retreat, Wolf Pen, Lover's Leap, Ghost Dance, Pluto's Cave, Alligator Rock, The Chain of Rocks, Devil's Workshop, and Honey Comb Rock. The principal canyon has walls nearly sixty feet high with a long narrow passageway.

Dixon Springs takes its name from William Dixon, one of the first white men to build a home in this section. A small community grew up at Dixon Springs with a general store, post office, blacksmith shop, grist mill, and several churches. The grist mill disappeared, but the other buildings continue to be used.

This region is rich in folklore and historic interest. The central valley contains a number of medicinal springs, the efficacy of whose waters was recognized by the Indians who maintained this area as neutral ground with the waters available to all tribes.

Dixon Springs became a nineteenth-century health spa, attracting hundreds to the seven springs of mineral-enriched water. A bathhouse provided mineral or soft water baths, both hot or cold, available at any time. The natural beauty of the area and its interesting stone formations, which helped to give the park valley a more equable temperature in the summer than most of southern Illinois, made the resort so popular that steamboat excursions were run from as far away as Paducah, Kentucky; Evansville, Indiana; and Cairo to Golconda, where a train took vacationers to within a couple of miles of the park.

Bold cliffs and beetling crags overhang the brook at Dixon Springs State Park in the Shawnee National Forest. *(Illinois Dept. of Conservation)*

LOCATION

The 496-acre park is about ten miles west of Golconda, on Route 146 near its junction with Route 145. The Brownfield (Illinois) 15′ USGS quad covers this area.

CLIMBING

This area is ideal for bouldering, a sport in itself in some parts of the climbing establishment. There are many rocks that contain short, extremely difficult bouldering problems, although there is little roped climbing.

John Gill did some bouldering there several years ago, despite the fact that there is nothing more than twenty-five feet high. Gill, to the neophyte climber who may not be familiar with the name, is almost synonymous with the term bouldering. His approach involves techniques that make him the master of the handhold, scaling small cliffs where 5.10 climbs leave off. According to Gill, "Bouldering is essentially severe one-pitch rock climbing, gracefully performed and completely protected. The setting is usually a low rock."

Dixon Springs is ideally suited to the challenge of bouldering.

ACCOMMODATIONS AND OTHER ATTRACTIONS

Facilities at Dixon Springs State Park are set up for swimming, picnicking, camping, and hiking.

Picnic tables and outdoor stoves are available at two shaded picnic areas, each with a playground and parking area. Drinking water is available.

A modern swimming pool provides swimmers with the protection of a lifeguard as well as bathhouse facilities. Towering oaks, elms, and birch trees shade the pool, built in 1957. A concession stand near the swimming pool dispenses a variety of refreshments.

There is a nature trail marked for more than a mile in the park, and a tent and trailer camping area with limited electricity and flush and pit toilets. See the ranger for a permit. A youth group camping area is also available, but groups of more than twenty-five persons need advance permission to enter the park.

For more details about this site, call or write Ranger, RR 1, Brownfield, Illinois 62911, (618) 949-3394.

There are motels in nearby Vienna and Golconda and private camp grounds in both towns. Steamboat Hill Campground, one-half mile northeast of Golconda on FR 411, has 31 rustic camp sites (no showers). In Vienna, Cedar Lake Ranch has 75 improved campsites with showers.

Mississippi Palisades State Park

DESCRIPTION

Mississippi Palisades State Park is located in a geologic division known as the Driftless Area. This unglaciated topography contains steep limestone bluffs, dissected by wooded ravines.

It is a popular training ground for a number of college climbing clubs, drawing climbers from Chicago and Iowa schools as well. Noted for its beautiful fossilized limestone bluffs that rise up from the Mississippi River, Mississippi Palisades State Park is a 1,717-acre complete recreation facility, with boating, fishing, and horseback riding. Fifteen miles of foot trails lead hikers to the crest of the Palisades and through other picturesque areas. Picnic areas with grills and tables near a refreshment concession house and camp ground are centrally located.

Persons interested in geology will find in the limes-

Massive sandstone formations form precipitous bluffs in Giant City State Park. *(Illinois Dept. of Conservation)*

tone rock formations an abundance of material for study. The deep wooded ravines are filled with ferns and the bases of the cliffs are dotted with uncommon plants found in no other place in that secion of Illinois.

The area within the park borders was once inhabited by a considerable Indian population, which left remnants of its culture upon the landscape. Numerous burial mounds are found within the park's boundary. These mounds are easily accessible by well-marked hiking trails. In order to preserve the natural beauty and historic sites, this land was acquired by the state of Illinois in 1929.

The name Palisades was given to the steep limestone bluffs along the Mississippi River because of the resemblance to similar geological formations on the Hudson River in New York. Bluffs and rock palisades overlooking the river, hillside prairies, and wooded uplands together provide a large area for various outdoor activities.

Vertical columns of rock bordering the Mississippi River form the park's western boundary. The Indian Head formation has a startling resemblance to the facial characteristics of an old Indian. A cliff farther north, in the form of a pair of tall separated columns, is called the Twin Sisters.

Most of the climbs are sixty feet high or less, with a few up to 120 feet, so most climbers practice their techniques using an overhead belay. However, most routes can be used as an alternative to top roping.

LOCATION

Mississippi Palisades State Park is located near the confluence of the Apple and Mississippi rivers in northwestern Illinois, about four miles north of Savanna, just off SH 84, in Carroll County. The USGS Savanna (Illinois) 15′ quadrangle covers this area.

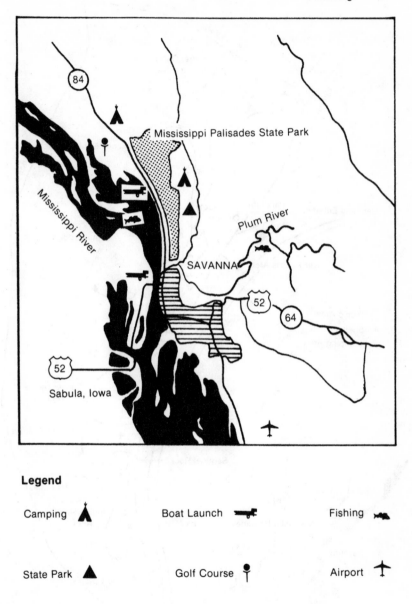

Legend

Camping

Boat Launch

Fishing

State Park

Golf Course

Airport

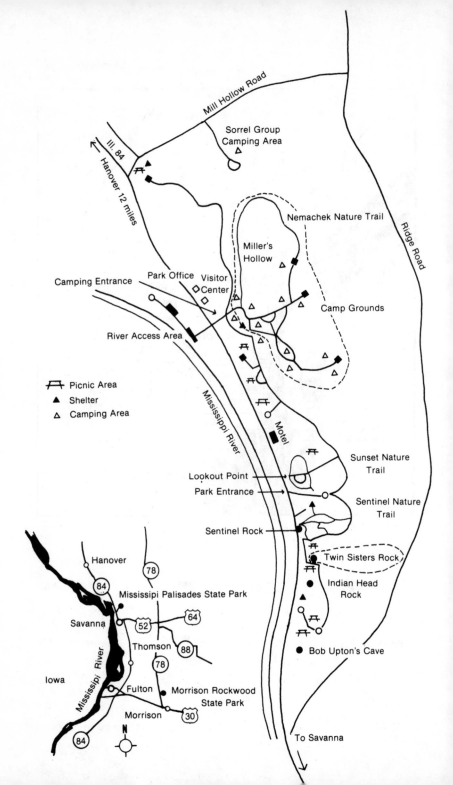

CLIMBING

The four popular climb sites at Mississippi Palisades are all within two large areas known by the names Twin Sisters and Sentinel. A regional guide booklet called the *Guide to Mississippi Palisades,* written by James Kolocotranis, describes thirty-one routes in the two areas. The booklet is available for about $2 plus postage from Pine Mountain Wilderness Equipment, 1529 S. Green River Rd., Evansville, IN 47715.

Most of the climbs at the Palisades are fairly easy, class 5.5 or less. All the difficult routes involve overhangs and are rated at "somewhere above 5.5."

Twin Sisters

This area derives its name from the two "twin" pillars of rock that form a chimney on a pedestal. Normally climbers start their route from the top of the pedestal from the east side. The climbs are all quite easy, with the exception of Difficult Crack and Horrendous.

Open Bible

Just north of the Twin Sisters proper, Open Bible has several good routes which combine a mixture of degrees of difficulty. Popover involves climbing a couple of overhangs and is a very popular route. The most difficult climb in this area is Horrific, a crack climb to a ledge, then an overhang.

Sentinel Area (West Face)

This area is located just a few feet from the unused, first road south of the main park entrance. Here, three one hundred twenty-foot routes make more interesting climbs. The West Face is a series of chimney climbs with three or four possible leads. An aid pitch adds interest. Nine bolts run diagonally left up to a ledge below the summit, which can be used with stirrups and tension (requires nine quarter-inch bolt hangers and nuts). The rest can be climbed free. One of the routes, Strenuous, can also be climbed with aid.

Sentinel Quadrangle (East Face)

A popular series of climbs located here is accessible by climbing from the road to the back of Sentinel. There is a variety of routes, including some unique chimney moves. Hellish Move and Fourth Crack are the most difficult moves because they involve overhangs.

ACCOMMODATIONS AND OTHER ATTRACTIONS

Tent and trailer facilities are available year round and include a modern utility building with showers and flush toilets. Electric hookups and a sanitary dump station are provided for contained units.

A group camping area is also available, but groups of more than twenty-five persons must have advance permission to enter the park. All campers must obtain a permit at the camp registration building before entering the camp ground.

Sorrel Campground, an area apart from the regular camp ground, is maintained for overnight horse camping and riders.

For day use, numerous picnic tables, water, and sanitary facilities are found throughout the park. Shelter houses and playgrounds are located at the main entrance.

Eleven miles of well-marked hiking trails span the park from the Mississippi River flood plain to the top of the Palisades. Trails atop the Palisades afford the hiker sweeping vistas of the Mississippi River. Lookout Point, easily accessible by automobile or hiking trail, has an observation platform built atop the bluffs. Some of the park trails closely parallel the bluff line.

Private camp grounds are available outside the park. Lakewood Resort, one mile north of the park on Millhollow Road, is open all year and offers a hundred sites, showers, and utility hookups.

A number of motels close to the park include Palisades Motel, Laws Motel, Off The Highway Motel, and Pine Lodge Motel.

Climbing Areas: Iowa (13 areas)
Backbone State Park (6 areas)
  Lower Picnic Area
  The Backbone:
    North End
    Middle Area
    South Bluffs
  Richmond Springs Bluffs
  Maquoketa River Cliffs
Palisades-Kepler State Park (3 areas)
  Lookout Tower
  Cliff Trail Area
  Quarry near the dam
Maquoketa Caves State Park
Ledges State Park (2 areas)
  Big Wall and Table Rock (Pease Creek)
  Sentinel Rock
Yellow River State Forest

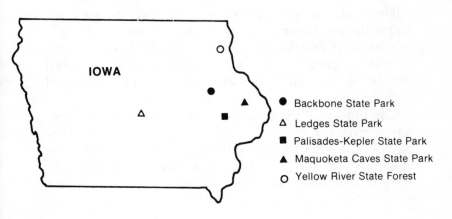

IOWA

● Backbone State Park
△ Ledges State Park
■ Palisades-Kepler State Park
▲ Maquoketa Caves State Park
○ Yellow River State Forest

Climbing in Iowa is done on the randomly occurring sandstone outcrops in the interior sections of the state. One of the most beautiful areas is Iowa's "Little Switzerland," which is named for its rugged beauty as the only unglaciated portion of northeastern Iowa. Delaware, Clayton and Allamakee counties make up the Little Switzerland area.

Iowa is a tableland that tilts gently upward from southeast to northwest. About 95 percent cultivated farmland (more than any other state, Iowa's bold bluffs mark the courses of some of its rivers. Climbing is done in four state parks geographically located in roughly the eastern half of Iowa. Here, fairly solid limestone outcrops provide cimbers with some good, usable routes in Ledges State Park, near Boone; Backbone State Park, near Dundee; Palisades-Kepler State Park near Mount Vernon; and Maquoketa Caves State Park, near Maquoketa. Climbing is also done at the Yellow River State Forest, near Waukon Junction.

The type of rock that makes up the climbable portions of the state is predominantly dolomite, a type of Silurian age limestone. Dolomite is found at Palisades-Kepler, Backbone, and Maquoketa Caves, but a younger (middle Pennsylvania) rock form, a channel sandstone, makes up the bedrock outcroppings at Ledges State Park.

There are no guidebooks on climbing in Iowa because the predominant activity is rapelling. The bluffs in most of the parks are ideally suited to this, but there is also a good number of climbing routes scattered throughout the state, centered in the parks described here.

Climbing is a fairly new sport to Iowa, when compared with the more popular (and perhaps more climbable) states surrounding it. Indeed, many people are surprised to find that Iowa has any climbing at all. This is not to say some of the parks are not crowded during peak summer months. In fact, Palisades-Kepler, perhaps the best-known climbing area in Iowa, is so crowded with rappelling enthusiasts that it is often difficult to climb to the top of some of the bluffs without bumping into someone coming down.

Iowa is sure to experience a good growth rate in popularity among Midwestern climbers once the word spreads, perhaps not among the most serious climbers, who will probably always prefer the excellent rock at Devil's Lake in Wisconsin, but to those more inclined to explore new areas.

Iowa will not leave the discoverers disappointed. In fact, with its many caves, rare plants, and accommodating campground system, it would be hard to find a more varied type of climbable terrain anywhere in the Midwest.

Backbone State Park

DESCRIPTION

Backbone State Park gets its name from a high ridge of dolomite (limestone) rock in the approximate center of the area. It bumps along for a quarter of a mile, closely resembling a huge backbone, with boulders and rocky humps forming its vertebrae.

Formerly called The Devil's Backbone, it is bounded by the Maquoketa River. The river flows southeast along the rock ledge, continues the length of it until it finds a saddle, goes through this, then turns to flow back almost northwest along the opposite side of the ledge. At times it's only a few hundred feet from the portion of the current flowing south.

The Backbone is the highest point in northeast Iowa. Covered with vegetation, the Backbone supports some fine pines and other trees. Wind-blown pines, resembling the famous Cypress Point trees of California, jut over the cliffs at several points. There are many rock

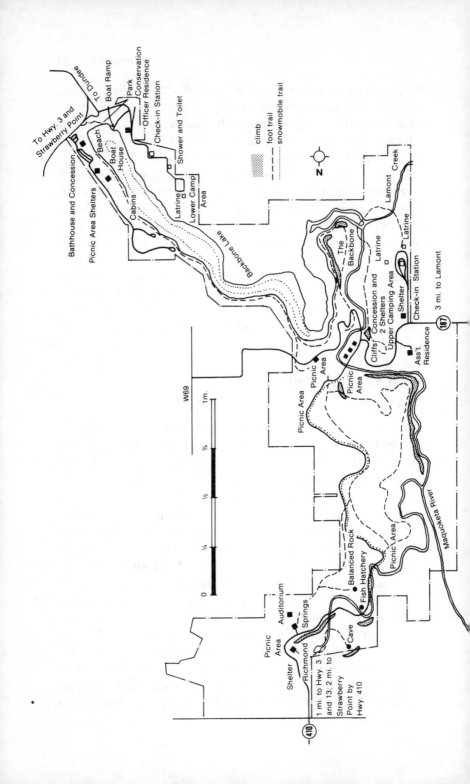

staircases and caverns at Backbone. The precipitous walls of the rocky ledges are favorites among climbers from many parts of the Midwest, since the park is close to Wisconsin's and Illinois' western borders.

Backbone State Park was dedicated October 1, 1919, with an area of thirteen hundred acres. Since then, it has grown to include sixteen hundred of the most scenic acres in the Midwest. Visitors not acquainted with Iowa beauty spots are due for a considerable surprise in Backbone. Within the park's borders will be found recreation including hiking, climbing, nature study, and a lake for swimming, boating, and fishing. There are trout streams, a trout hatchery well worth a visit, an auditorium capable of seating a few hundred persons, cabins, shelters, natural beauty galore for photography buffs, and picnic tables. All these make for a pleasant stay, whether it's for two weeks or just a day's outing.

The romantic history of the park is filled with tales of Indian battles, train and bank robbers, cattle rustlers, and horse thieves, all of whom may have used the Backbone for hiding. These tall tales (some true) make good listening when told by those who have visited the park for several years.

Just outside the park is a conservation commission pine forest attractive to photographers and, in season, bow hunters. A conservation officer and his assistant, as well as fish hatchery personnel, live in the park all year. Campers or those desiring to rent cabins must register with the park officer or his assistant.

Many of the trails Backbone has to offer are marked, and hikers will have no trouble finding one to their liking.

LOCATION

Backbone State Park sits off SH 410, five miles southwest of Strawberry Point in the northwest corner of Delaware County. The towns of Lamont and Dundee, both seven miles southwest of the park, have shopping centers, motels, and other facilities. Backbone is included on the USGS Dundee and Strawberry Point (Iowa) 7½′ quadrangles.

There are six climbing sites at the park, three located around the Backbone itself, another north of the main picnic area in about the middle of the park, one on the north side of the Maquoketa River, and another near Richmond Springs. There are a few entrances to the park, from all directions. The shortest route through the park is to take either County Road (CR) W-69 from the east or SH 187 from the west to the center of the park, where you will find a large picnic area and a concession stand with two shelters. On the other side of the river (to the east) from the shelter is a parking lot, and a foot trail leads to the Backbone. The trail loops around the rocks and connects with other trails that go to opposite ends of the park.

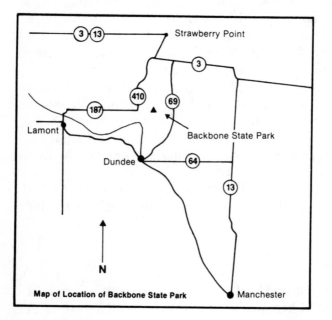

Map of Location of Backbone State Park

Lower Picnic Area

Closest to the Lamont (west) entrance to the park is the climbing area known as the Lower Picnic Area, or primitive camp ground, since there is a camp ground nearby which is suitable for tent camping but has no utility hookups for trailers. Here the cliffs are seventy to ninety feet high and stretch around the Maquoketa River for about a quarter mile. The road from the Lamont entrance dips here about a hundred feet from the level of the plateau surrounding the Lamont area. This dip gives rise to the eroded bluffs that form the climbing site. The cliffs are sheer faces of limestone, set back in the bush, accessible by a vague, brushy path beginning at the parking lot below.

To get to these cliffs, follow the park road from the Lamont entrance for about a half mile to a parking lot on the left-hand side of the road (before getting to the "T" in the park road). Cross the road and follow the trail that leads to the cliffs, which are clearly visible from the lot.

The path leads through a thicket that passes around the cliffs and angles off to the right. Circle around on this path to the top and over the cliffs to where a top rope can be lowered at various places. The view is spectacular from the top, overlooking much of the park. More direct routes through a few passes are accessible, but necessitate climbing fifty- to sixty-degree inclines.

There are some good leads up the rock faces all along the cliffs. There are at least fifteen good routes here, many of them quite difficult. The climbing ranges in degree of difficulty from some rolling twenty-five foot walls for beginners to quite advanced table-rock formations that tower close to the river, at the far end of the trail. These offer the more advanced climber some good F8 and F9 routes, with a couple of aid climbs toward the far end of the trail where the river gets really close to the bank (following the river south about a half mile).

THE BACKBONE: NORTH END

The park's most prominent geological formation, The Backbone, is easy to locate. From the Lamont park entrance, follow the park road to the junction of SH 410 and turn right up the steep hill that leads to a parking lot with a large stone monument holding a sign which reads "The Backbone." Park here and walk up the trail. The pathway narrows about fity yards down the trail. Here, where the land narrows between the Maquoketa River and the impoundment known as Backbone Lake to the left (east), you'll find two steep rock walls that are solid limestone. The space, only about four feet wide, makes an excellent climbing area. Either wall can be climbed after dropping down from the top.

THE BACKBONE: MIDDLE AREA

By following the trail that runs on top of the walls about a hundred yards from the start of the trail head, you'll come to the middle area of the Backbone with its blend of half walls and half rock formations (straight walls and concave sections of rock). From these you can rappel free and drop into the reservoir below for a bit of added excitement on a hot summer day. The fifty- to sixty-foot high rocks demand that you pick and choose carefully where you drop over the side on a rappel. Some places are impossible to climb back up and you'll end up walking the shoreline of the river or reservoir back to the trail head.

Not too much climbing is done in this middle area. Rapelling is a very popular activity here, with climbers rappelling down and scrambling back up an easy, more rolling section of rock to the top.

THE BACKBONE: SOUTH BLUFFS

It is only one mile from the trail head to the south end of the Backbone and some excellent bluff climbing, but it is hard to get to (even over the trail) because of the dense undergrowth. The trai bumps up and down like a roller coaster, over rugged rocks that are hard to walk on. But the sheer walls and table rocks are the best climbing on the whole Backbone. Because of erosion, the bluff structure is constantly changing, making it a shifting area where the climbing may sometimes be rendered inaccessible. Here, sixty-foot face climbs that drop to the river below are both exciting and challenging.

Richmond Springs Bluffs

The cliffs on the north side of the park, near Richmond Springs, are very hard to reach by foot, but the climbs are well worth the effort. The bluffs can be seen from the road, easily at certain times of the year and just glimpsed in summer when heavy foliage hides them from view.

Nearest the north park entrance (from Strawberry Point) is the park road leading to the bluffs, not more than three-eighths of a mile into the park. There is a parking lot near a picnic grounds, with a shelter on the west side of the road. The cliffs face the south, adjacent to the road, and can be reached by hiking from the picnic shelter.

Despite the tough accessibility, the climbs on the north side are some of the best, with some very high walls (at least fifty to sixty feet and some as many as ninety feet high). The very good routes must be explored (best done in the fall or spring when there are no leaves to restrict vision), because there are no guidebooks on any of Iowa's climbing areas.

Here, as with most other remote rock climbing areas,

it's a good idea to keep a sharp eye out for hazards such as beehives in the rocks, poisonous snakes sunning themselves on the rocks, and poison ivy. There are rattlers at Backbone, but they are generally small and relatively few in number.

Maquoketa River Cliffs

This area is perhaps the longest ridge of high ground in the park and consists of about a mile of forty- to seventy-foot cliffs on the north and east side of the Maquoketa River, abutting its banks. The Maquoketa River Cliffs offer good solid rock for those who don't mind hiking to get there. A path running along the river bank below and several trails—mostly deer trails—snake their way around the top rim of the bluffs. After the first freeze and the leaves change colors, the area is exceptionally beautiful. It is tough walking on the top trails unless the dense undergrowth has thinned out.

The best climbing routes are scattered along the mile-long ridge, with marginal areas intermingled with excellent climb sites. It is easy to see them from the riverbed, so it's best to hike in along the bottom.

Rappelling may be the most popular activity among climbers at Backbone, but along this set of cliffs are some good free climbs in the moderate (F6) range. There are a few table rocks and many sheer faces of solid limestone with almost no cracks or breaks.

ACCOMMODATIONS AND OTHER ATTRACTIONS

The park has both camp grounds and cabins within its boundaries, the cabins offering an economical alternative to area motels for those who don't wish to camp. The cabins are modern and sleep four comfortably. Cots are supplied for additional guests at the rate of about 50¢ a day, per person. The cabins can be rented by the week, through reservations placed with the park officials. The cost per cabin is approximately $80 a week. Renters provide their own bedding and linen.

Camping facilities include 410 sites, about a tenth of them with electricity. The park is open all year, although showers and water supplies may not be connected during winter months.

Private camp ground facilities include the 27-site Forest Villa Resort, located two miles north of Dundee on CR W-69 at Backbone State Park Beach, and the 50-site Double J Campground, a mile west of Edgewood on SH 3.

There is a public park in Manchester, Pin Oak-Maquoketa River Access County Park, 2 miles southeast of Manchester on U.S. Route 20, which has 50 campsites.

Three motels are available in Manchester: Sleepy Hollow Motel, Broadlawn Motel, and Cozy Rest Motel.

Palisades-Kepler State Park

DESCRIPTION

Palisades-Kepler State Park covers 688 acres along the banks of the Cedar River, in Linn County, near Cedar Rapids. Vertical cliffs along the river, dotted with moss, ferns, and swallows' nests, add to the natural beauty of the scenic area. The name comes from combining the outstanding geological features of the park, the palisades along the river, with the Kepler family name. The Keplers were among the original donors of land.

Indian mounds within the park area were found to contain ancient pottery, stone fishhooks, and arrows. These mounds were gleaned many years ago and now most of these Indian relics may be seen in museums across the state.

Palisades-Kepler State Park contains a variety of natural beauty, enhanced by trees, shrubs, and woody vines which shelter the well-marked trails that wind through the park. Lookout Tower, close to two climbing areas at the park, furnishes a view of the limestone cliffs used by climbers, primarily to rappel. The Cedar River, which winds its way through the surrounding countryside, forms the park's western boundary.

The tower is upstream from the parking area and is accessible by a trail. The climbing areas can also be reached by this trail or another foot trail farther upstream. Cool breezes off the river offering relief from the scorching Iowa summers make the tower a main attraction on hot days.

The park is heavily wooded and contains a couple of interesting stone cabins built during the 1930s by the Civilian Conservation Corps (CCC). The cabins are available to rent (see "Accommodations").

LOCATION

Palisades-Kepler is located on the USGS Mount Vernon (Iowa) 7½' quadrangle. The park is near the town of Mount Vernon, in Linn County, about eight miles east of Cedar Rapids. The only entrance is off U.S. Route 30 from the northeast.

CLIMBING

There are three climbing areas at Palisades-Kepler, all on the Cedar River, fairly close to each other. They are the Lookout Tower, the Cliff Trail area, and the small quarry near the dam at the south end of the park. Dolomite is the bedrock type found here, with its faces and cracks the predominant formations to climb.

While rappelling is no doubt the most popular activity, the serious rock climber will find jam crack techniques the most useful. Although the bluffs overlooking the river are not sheer, they offer a series of changing faces rising at points to eighty feet high, while at other points the bluffs are only forty feet in height. The cliffs are usually crowded with rappellers on summer weekends, but the area makes an excellent practice site for nearly all kinds of climbing throughout the year.

There is good climbing variety, with a little bit of everything: faces, slabs, overhangs, caves, cracks, laybacks, mantle shelves, and traverses. Most of the climbs here are moderately hard, but all can be done free. Aid climbing must be approached very carefully because the soft limestone rock is rotten in some places.

LOOKOUT TOWER

A large cavern here makes it one of the nicest climb spots in the park. If rappelled, the wall goes down about twenty feet and opens into a cave over which you can free fall the rest of the way to the bottom. On the way up, is a window through the side (almost like a chimney) that makes a little tunnel you can climb through. There are many different routes around the window, so take your pick. The overhang is rated about F9.

Nearby, about thirty yards to the north of the cavern, are some eighty-foot high bluffs (about one hundred fifty yards to the north of the Lookout Tower itself). These bluffs contain some of the most difficult climbs.

CLIFF TRAIL AREA

Starting at the Tower, and either following the top of the bluffs north along the foot trail (shown on the park maps as the Cliff Trail) or taking the trail that goes to the bluffs north of the family cabins, you will come to another area known locally as The Bitch. It is about one hundred fifty yards north of the eighty-foot high bluffs and is reached by climbing down through a valley and back up the other side. There are some

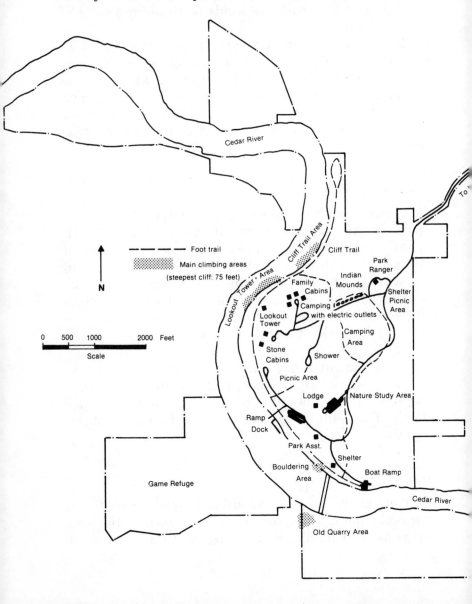

excellent climbs here, but you'll just have to search for what looks good. There are no guidebooks with step-by-step descriptions and the choices here are many. Another smaller area down through another valley and across a small footbridge is also a good place to look for climbs.

The main hiking trail connects all these areas from above, but you can also walk along the river's edge at the bottom of the bluffs during most of the summer. At other times of the year, the river is normally too high, and the shoreline, visible in summer, is covered with water. During the summer, about a three or four-foot ledge is all that is exposed to either begin a climb or end a rappel, so the climbs are most accessible from the top. Most climbs are top roped anyway.

QUARRY AREA NEAR THE DAM

There are two more climb sites south of the tower. One is a bouldering area near the dam in what is known as the lower Palisades area (directly south of the assistant park superintendent's home). The rock wall near the dam on the east side of the river is a good practice area for rappelling. A bigger and better area, accessible only by crossing the river in a boat, is situated on the southwest bank near the dam. It is an old rock face that was created to repair the dam in 1961.

The face was blasted out to provide limestone that was placed in the river to help bolster the aging dam. Sheer cliffs created by the blasting are about eighty-feet high and quite solid. The walls are fairly narrow, up to perhaps three hundred feet in length. But climbers can scale the south and east walls, using crack or face-climbing techniques, and spend most of the day here.

The site is visible from the park (east) shore and can be studied with binoculars before crossing the river.

To get to the quarry, cross the river on the upstream side of the dam. There are numerous places to secure a boat on the west shore. (Boats are not presently available for rent at the park so you'll have to bring your own. There is a dock and ramp at the park, however.) After landing, walk inland about a hundred feet and start the climb on the wall.

There are plans for a boat concession which could go into effect during the next year or two. There is also state legislation pending that would appropriate money to build a new dam, which would then allow easier access to the quarry.

ACCOMMODATIONS AND OTHER ATTRACTIONS

Two stone cabins built by the CCC in the 1930s are available for rent and make ideal facilities during the cool fall days of October. Working fireplaces and the colorful autumn view from the bluffs overlooking the Cedar River make this a charming attraction. Each cabin sleeps eight and rents for about $80 a week. There are also four modern family cabins that each sleep four and have the same rent. Reservations can be made through the park superintendent.

Two camping areas, one with electricity and another more primitive area, are located within the park boundaries. A typical nightly camping fee is charged and permits must be secured from the park office. Water, showers, dump stations, and toilet facilities are provided at both camp grounds, as are tables and fireplaces. The park ranger's address is RR2, Mount Vernon, Iowa 52314, (319) 895-6039.

Motel accommodations are available in Cedar Rapids and Marion, and a number of private camp grounds surround the park.

Squaw Creek Park has a 45-site camp ground located two miles southeast on U.S. 151 and SH 13. Lake

Macbride State Park, in Solon, also has 200 modern and rustic campsites, some with electricity, nestled among its 382 acres of forest.

Linn County is part of the Hawkeye Scenic Circle drive that is famous for its historical richness. A few highlights of the tour are listed here. Seminole Valley and Squaw Creek parks have restored houses from the 1880s. Check with the chamber of commerce, 127 Third Street, NE, Cedar Rapids, Iowa 52404, for specific information as well as available tours.

Marion is the original county seat, dating back to 1837. You might enjoy driving the quiet streets, viewing old, historic homes or searching for old markers in Oak Shade Cemetery.

Perhaps the most unique town in the county is Whittier, north of Marion on SH 13 and east a few miles on CR E-34. This quiet Quaker village of some two hundred inhabitants is a part of the oldest Quaker group in the United States, which numbers only two thousand. A Quaker meeting house is located in Whittier and services may be visited on any Sunday at 10 A.M.

Maquoketa Caves State Park

DESCRIPTION

Maquoketa Caves State Park contains less than a half mile of surfaced road; the rest of the way is by foot on well-marked, though sometimes rugged, trails. The center of the 192-acre park is a steep ravine with sheer cliffs ranging from ten to seventy-five feet in height. Trails leading around the top of these cliffs to lookouts offering views of the valley are quite exciting.

In the spring the whole area is carpeted with hepaticas; summer entertains a profusion of wildflowers everywhere; and fall brings out the bright orange of bittersweet that has been known to climb a tall white

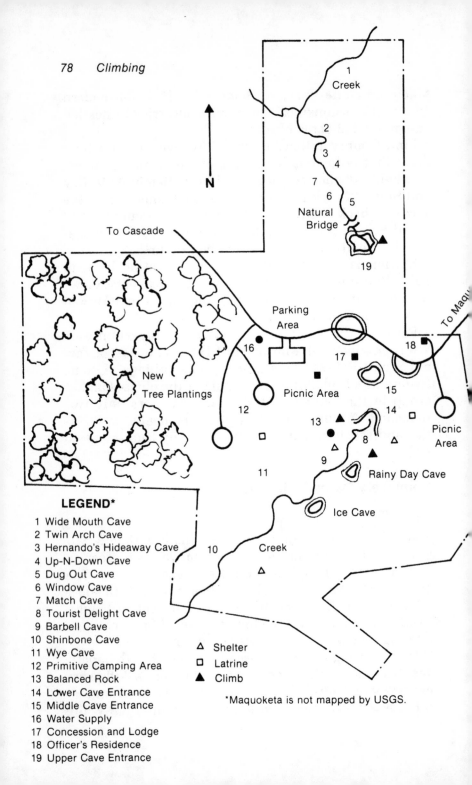

LEGEND*

1 Wide Mouth Cave
2 Twin Arch Cave
3 Hernando's Hideaway Cave
4 Up-N-Down Cave
5 Dug Out Cave
6 Window Cave
7 Match Cave
8 Tourist Delight Cave
9 Barbell Cave
10 Shinbone Cave
11 Wye Cave
12 Primitive Camping Area
13 Balanced Rock
14 Lower Cave Entrance
15 Middle Cave Entrance
16 Water Supply
17 Concession and Lodge
18 Officer's Residence
19 Upper Cave Entrance

△ Shelter
□ Latrine
▲ Climb

*Maquoketa is not mapped by USGS.

pine until it appears to be decorated for Christmas. Winter snows cover the evergreen and aspen with soft beauty, while gnarled cedars in clefts of rock on the cliffs appear as ghostly sentinels.

Thirteen named caves honeycomb the valley and are of much interest to spelunkers. A ranger lives in the park to care for it and its caves. There is a concession stand for refreshments and information about the caves and trails.

Maquoketa Caves became a state park in 1921, but there is plenty of evidence that the caves were used by sightseers long before that. Not only are initials and names carved in the limestone walls of the caves and cliffs that date back to 1835, but Indian pottery, arrowheads, spears, and other relics show that these caverns may have been home to tribes who lived hundreds—perhaps thousands—of years ago.

When first discovered by a hunting party before the Civil War, the cave ceilings were hung with beautiful, milk-white stalactites with corresponding stalagmites rising from the floor. Souvenir hunters have robbed the caves of their rarest beauty, yet much of the unique, attractive, and fascinating formation still remains.

Electric lights are strung through the major caves, and pathways are easily followed. Some of the other caverns, like Hernando's Hideaway, Ice Cave, Rainy Day, Window, and Shinbone necessitate the use of a good flashlight, as does Bat Passage and the exciting Steel Gate Passage, which open off the main cave. The park ranger will be glad to tell you about any of the caves, most of which are plainly marked by signs.

LOCATION

Maquoketa Caves State Park is located about seven miles west of the city of Maquoketa, on CR E-17, in the southwest corner of Jackson County. Take U.S. Route

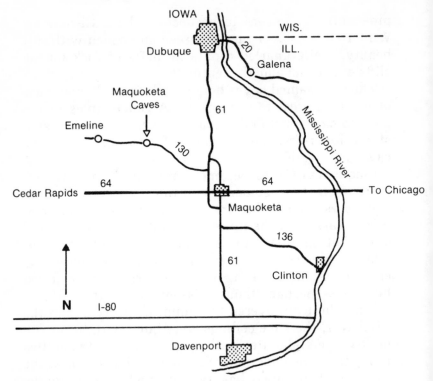

61 north to intersect with E-17. Signs from U.S. Route 61 on the north side of Maquoketa will aid in directing you to the park.

There is no USGS quad mapping for this area.

CLIMBING

Maquoketa Caves is a small park with numerous rolling hills covered by woodlands and bluffs. The small river valley has climbable bluffs on both sides. Top-roped climbing is the thing here and rappelling is more popular than route finding, primarily because of the nature of the limestone bluffs; they are difficult to climb because of the sheer, fairly smooth faces and the fair amount of loose rock which makes people a bit uneasy.

It is hard work scaling many of the walls at Maquoketa while others are very easy, so it seems like there is no middle ground. Most of the climbing is exposed face climbing: start at the bottom of the ledges and find any handholds you can. There are many cliffs and bluffs throughout the park, and many trails leading to them. Trails are marked but are not shown on the park maps available at the superintendent's office. Climbers can easily spend more than a day at the park and never climb the same place twice. The cliffs are not very good for hardware because the limestone is too soft, but there are plenty of trees at the top from which to anchor a belay or set up a rappel line. Care should obviously be given to the flora when using trees as anchors.

There are more than twenty caves in the park (most of them small) with underground systems. Some of the caves just barely meet the definition of having at least twenty-five feet of undercut bank.

Dance Hall Cave, the major and largest cave in the park, marks a popular climbing site. The cave cuts under the park road; it is below the traffic. The cave goes in well past a hundred feet, and other caves join off this main passageway.

To reach Dance Hall Cave, drive or walk past the ranger station and bear right on the paved road off the county (park) highway. The cave is at the right and you can see its big mouth from the road. It is marked with a sign and is close to the concession and park information stand.

A spectacular rappel over the mouth of this cave is nearly ninety feet in height. At the top, a three-inch ledge is all there is to stand on. Just jump out over the ledge and free hang all the way down.

Most of the higher pitches in the park (eighty or ninety feet) are undercut like this one, although there are some free-climb sites scattered throughout the rest of the park. The undercut portions lean out from the main rocks and are very difficult to climb.

ACCOMMODATIONS AND OTHER ATTRACTIONS

The park offers 50 rustic sites in the central camp grounds. For tent and trailer camping, no reservations are needed, but campers must secure a permit from the park office. A daily fee is charged and camping is limited to two weeks.

As with all Iowa state parks, a basic camping unit is defined as the portable shelter used by one to six persons. Only one vehicle may be used for transportation in the camp area. All other motor vehicles must be parked in the visitor parking area and so marked. Persons over the basic unit of six are charged a nominal additional amount. Space, water, and sanitary facilities are included in the campsite fee. No charge is made for the use of the picnic areas. Fireplaces, tables, and running water are provided for picnicking.

Motels are available in Maquoketa, and eight camp grounds within a fifteen-mile radius from the park also serve as accommodations. In Bellevue, Bellevue State Park has 100 sites (with showers); Pleasant Creek Public Use Area, run by the U.S. Army Corps of Engineers (COE), has 25 rustic sites; and Spruce Creek Park has 60 rustic sites (half of them with utilities). There are 150 campsites (showers) at Central Park in Center Junction and 10 campsites at Bulgers Hollow Public Use Area (COE), off U.S. Route 67 near Clinton.

Bloomfield Park on U.S. 61 in DeWitt has 10 sites. Massillon Area Park in Massillon, off U.S. 30, has 20 sites and Miles Roadside Park on SH 64 has 15 sites.

Ledges State Park

DESCRIPTION

Outstanding among Ledges State Park's 900 acres of scenic attractions and unusual rock formations is the Ledges, from which the park name was derived. These ledges are bluffs of sandstone channel fillings of the Cherokee group, Pennsylvanian in age. These miniature sandstone cliffs, from twenty-five to seventy-five feet high, border Pease Creek, named in honor of one of the prominent pioneer settlers in that vicinity.

According to geologists, this area was once topographically high. It was then buried by glacial deposits, which are now being removed by erosion. The streams flowing through the park have eroded the softer glacial deposits, leaving the more resistant, relatively narrow valleys with steep sides.

Trails lead up and down steep slopes to scenic overlooks where the regional flora can be better observed. The Ledges hold many giant maples, cottonwoods, and ash. Some rare species of plants, such as closed gentian, walking ferns, pussytoes, and the rare showy orchis, are found here. The Des Moines River flows through the western edge of the park and has an excellent boat ramp, providing easy access to the park.

There are some interesting Indian mounds also within hiking distance of the park, including the Indian Council Ledge where, according to legend, chiefs and warriors of the Sioux, and later the Sac, Fox, and other tribes, gathered to boast of their wars. A guard was placed on the cliff known as Sentinel Rock, to watch for enemies, since the spot commands a view for miles in every direction.

LOCATION

Ledges State Park is located six miles south of the city of Boone, on SH 164, in central Boone County. The park is listed on the intersection of four USGS 7½′ quadrangles: Boone East and West, Madrid NW, and Luther. Many signs on the area roads wil help direct you to the park. The main entrance is three miles west from SH 17. There are two climbing sites: the Ledges

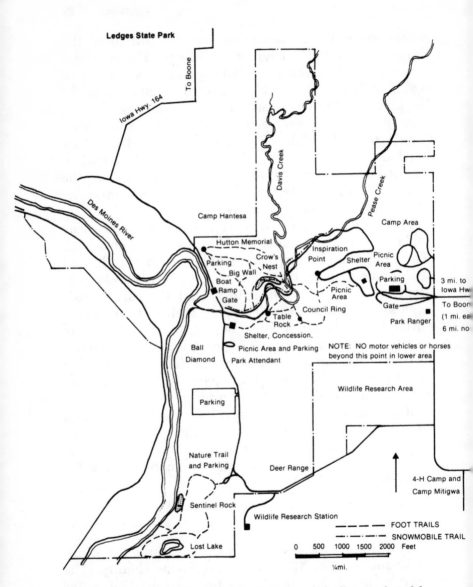

themselves, with the Big Wall (Main Bluffs) and Table Rock on either side of the main park road, and Sentinel Rock, at the southwest corner of the park. Sentinel Rock is reached by hiking over a nature trail near the Des Moines River.

CLIMBING

The main climbing areas at Ledges State Park are the Big Wall of the Ledges and the Table Rock, some fifty yards away from the Ledges. Both are in the central part of the park.

The Big Wall contains some 50-foot high faces consisting of rocks that are difficult climbing. Rappelling down and prussiking back up is a very popular activity there, although there are easy walking routes to the top of the climb sites. Something unique to this area is the Wallcleaners, a group of climbers from Iowa State University. On weekends they often set up a "zip line" and invite other climbers to join them in sliding across Pease Creek down the steep roped incline at the Big Wall.

Pease Creek runs through the park and flows through the Ledges and past the Table Rock formation. Table Rock is about fifty yards south of the Big Wall and around the bend in the creek. It rises a hundred feet in the air and is very popular for rappelling. A two-pitch rappel is necessary to get down the whole formation, since the route twists around the rock. You can walk paths to the top of Table Rock to set up a belay.

There are other cliffs in the main park area, but they are only twenty or thirty feet tall and separate from the Big Wall area.

Sentinel Rock, rising about sixty-five feet above the Des Moines River, is hard to reach because thick brush in the park trail blocks easy access. To reach the trail leading to the rock, drive to the southwest edge and park in the area marked "Lost Lake Nature Trail." Bear right at the fork in the trail and head toward the river. You'll see the Sentinel Rock, rising about sixty-five feet above the Des Moines River, is hard to reach because thick brush in the park trail blocks easy access. To reach the trail leading to the rock, drive to the

The Big Wall ledges of rock that hug Pease Creek give Ledges State Park its name. *(Lisa Kruidenier)*

southwest edge and park in the area marked "Lost Lake Nature Trail." Bear right at the fork in the trail and head toward the river. You'll see the Sentinel Rock formation on your right.

Accommodations and Other Attractions

Camping in Ledges State Park features 100 sites, 60 with electricity. Showers are available. A fee is charged for camping.

Other camp grounds are located in a twenty-mile radius from the park. McHose Roadside Park, located in Boone, has 10 sites available. Bells Mill Park in Stratford has 50 sites. Story City's Whispering Oaks KOA has 75 modern sites and many facilities. There are 150 sites at Spring Lake Campground, near Grand Junction, and 75 sites at Little Wall Lake Campgrounds, near Jewell. The largest camp ground in the area is the Lewis J. Lester County Park, with 500 sites. None of the parks other than Ledges has shower facilities.

Motels are fairly easy to find in Boone and Ames, unless Iowa State has a football game that weekend.

At the east edge of Ledges State Park is the Iowa Wildlife Research Station, which offers a free exhibit of animals native to Iowa, including birds and reptiles.

Yellow River State Forest

DESCRIPTION

One of the most picturesque regions in the United States is in the heart of northeast Iowa: the timbered hills and valleys of the Yellow River State Forest, north of McGregor.

Maintained by the Iowa State Conservation Commission, the Yellow River Forest features about twenty-five miles of backpacking trails, a couple of water sources, and free primitive camping, both in organized camp grounds and off-trail campsites for backpackers. This 5,800 acre forest is located in the midst of spectacular bluffs along the Mississippi River. The area offers outdoor recreation in Iowa's most natural form.

In the Paint Creek unit, sheer limestone bluffs, clear trout streams, wildlife, and quiet beauty punctuate acres of native timber. This timbered area has two bubbling trout streams, Big Paint and Little Paint creeks. Campers at the Paint Creek unit go to sleep by the gurgling cold water and can awaken to take a quiet walk along one of the creeks where they might chance upon a deer stopping for a drink. In Indian days, this region was a utopia for wild turkeys, but they were exterminated by the white settlers. Turkeys have been successfully reintroduced and the population is again building.

Bluff tops ring the north side of the unit. Here a sawmill is operated by the forestry section of the Iowa Conservation Commission. The state sawmill, near the forest headquarters, is active year round, although most sawing is done during winter months. When trees are marked for cutting, all possible products are considered. In a normal year, such things as veneer logs, barrel-stave bolts, railroad tie cuts, and pulpwood will all be sold from the forest area to commercial outlets. Most logs are brought to the sawmill, and the lumber produced is used by various sections of the conservation commission.

The Paint Creek unit of the Yellow River Forest is a planned area where the visitor enjoys the views and natural benefits, such as hunting and fishing near his

P	Picnic Area
□	Public Recreation Area
—·—·—	Bridle Trail
— — —	Foot Trail
X	Main and Best Public Access
▲	Passage Unsuitable with Trailers
H	Trail Ride Group Area

campsite, while at the same time development projects, commercial forest operations, game management, and research go on at the same time. Pine plantings edging the camp ground and the picnic area can be seen from the bluffs.

A drive south from the sawmill on a narrow, winding road takes you to Iowa's first fire tower. Continuing on this road eventually takes you to Iowa 76 toward Waukon and east to SH 364, toward Waukon Junction and Harpers Ferry, old river towns rich in history. Pioneer explorations of Marquette and Joliet and Zebulon Pike, Indian battles, fur traders, and tales of the Mississippi River are a few examples of this region's great past.

LOCATION

One of five state forests in Iowa, the Yellow River Forest is located in the southeast corner of Allamakee County, fourteen miles southeast of Waukon Junction on SH 76. The USGS Prairie du Chien (Wisconsin) 15′ quadrangle covers this area.

CLIMBING

Limestone bluffs make for a good variety of climbs in this forest. Many are sheer running faces up to eighty or ninety feet in height. The climbing is similar to that of the Mississippi Palisades in Illinois, and the rock is the same type of limestone as the upper Iowa River.

Some crack climbing is possible, since the bluffs vary in height from forty to ninety feet. Some pitches are very difficult when free climbing isn't possible, but aids often are not secure enough in the limestone, so be careful where you use them. Most of the climbing is easy to moderate in difficulty.

Many people would rather rappel than climb, because the limestone face often doesn't lend itself to scaling and rappelling seems more fun and less work.

ACCOMMODATIONS AND OTHER ATTRACTIONS

There are two camp grounds in the Yellow River State Forest that can accommodate vehicles with camper trailers, as well as tenters. There are also numerous off-trail campsites that backpackers usually prefer. There is no fee to camp here. Rustic-type facilities such as pit toilets and no showers are the order of the day.

There are also a few other parks with camping facilities in the general area. Pikes Peak State Park, three miles southeast of McGregor on SH 340, has 125 sites, some with electricity and showers. A private camp ground called Spook Cave, near McGregor, has 100 sites.

Clear Creek Ranch, two miles west of Lansing on SH 9, has 110 sites, with showers, and Gateway City Park, in Monona, has 18 sites.

Motels are available in Monona and Decorah.

Effigy Mounds National Monument, Iowa's only national monument, is located three miles north of Marquette on SH 76. This 1,352-acre area was established to preserve a group of ancient Indian burial mounds. At the visitor's center, a short slide program is presented on the history of the mounds and the Indians who made them. A pleasant walk takes visitors to the mounds and a scenic view of the Mississippi River. The visitor center is open from 8 A.M. to 5 P.M. daily, or 8 to 6, June through August.

About thirteen miles from the forest, Pikes Peak State Park is the highest bluff on the Mississippi. Available to visitors are camping, hiking trails, scenic views of the river, picnicking, refreshments, shelter, and sanitary facilities. Visitors may also view the park's Indian burial mounds.

At Harper's Ferry and Marquette, tourists can cross the Mississippi River. River trips are also offered.

Climbing Areas: Michigan
Porcupine Mountains State Park
Norwich Ledge
Grand Ledge

Michigan's mitten-shaped Lower Peninsula, 277 miles long and 195 miles wide, is relatively low and rolling, with countless lakes and marshes. From the flat plains in the southeast and the Saginaw lowlands, it rises to a moderate plateau in the north.

The Upper Peninsula is more rugged, with hills rising from the flat southeastern tip. Those in the south are low, but the range along the north coast of Lake Superior creates picturesque cliffs, some of the highest elevations in the state. Three ridges angle

MICHIGAN

Porcupine Mountains
■ State Park
▲ Norwich Ledge
● Grand Ledge

through the western part of the peninsula into Wisconsin and pour forth a wealth of copper and iron ore.

Because of the lack of many suitable outcrops of solid rock in Michigan, climbing is limited to a brief stretch of rocky escarpment on the shores of Lake Superior, known as the Porcupine Mountains Wilderness State Park, and to Grand Ledge, near Lansing.

Located approximately seventeen miles west of the town of Ontonagon in Michigan's Upper Peninsula, Porcupine Mountains, with 58,171 acres, is one of the few remaining large wilderness areas in the Midwest. Adjacent to the park on its south boundary are approximately three hundred square miles of the Ottawa National Forest, with its multitude of outdoor activities. Here another area, a long cliff structure of basalt (volcanic) rock, is accessible by a bushwhack through the brush between Norwich and Victoria, south of the town of Ontonagon.

Much more civilized is the Grand Ledge area, where a city park surrounds the climbing alons the walls of the Grand River. The sandstone bluffs at Grand Ledge are of the type of rock that crops out locally from beneath the glacial material that blankets much of the southern part of the state. The Pennsylvania-age sandstone here is a classic example of cyclic deposition in the Saginaw Formation, which has its chief outcrops near Grand Ledge.

All three areas are detailed in the following sections.

Porcupine Mountains State Park

DESCRIPTION

Towering stands of virgin timber, four secluded lakes, and miles of wild rivers and streams combine to make a trip to the "Porkies" one to remember. Porcupine Mountains State Park is formed by a rugged ridge of hills, with steep grades and stream crossings encountered at many locations. The trails traverse the various sections of the park and lead the hiker to spectacular lookouts and vistas. The Michigan Department of Natural Resources (DNR) maintains more than eighty miles of foot trails, rustic trailside cabins, and Adirondack shelters for public use.

Porcupine Mountains State Park was established in 1945 by the Michigan legislature. Since that time the Porkies have remained relatively unchanged. The remoteness of the interior, coupled with the stands of towering hemlock and pine, seems to defy time. Backpackers enjoy the remoteness of the park's interior section and find it as rugged as some parts of the West.

The park is open all year and is also used by skiers and deer hunters in winter. Park roads may not be plowed during deer season and the South Boundary Road and SH 107, beyond the ski area, are not plowed at all during winter.

The group of hills that give the park its name stand a thousand to fourteen hundred feet above Lake Superior. This is the western anchor of the Copper Range, extending northeasterly across Ontonagon County through the towns of Nonsuch, White Pine, Norwich, Victoria, Rockland, Caledonia, Mass, Greenland, and Lake Mine. Headwaters of many of the smaller rivers flowing into Lake Superior are found in this area.

Beautiful waterfalls cascade over the rocks near the Carp and Presque Isle rivers at the southwest end of the park. The remote hiking trails lead to some fine back-country lakes, rivers, streams, and ponds, and offer beautiful sights for the traveler.

LOCATION

Porcupine Mountains State Park straddles two counties and is located on the junction of four 15′ USGS topographic map quadrangles. The park itself takes up

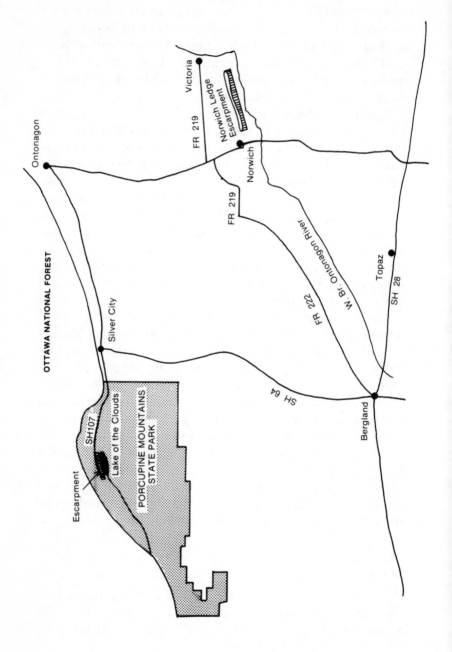

more than fifty thousand acres, which makes it the largest state park listed in this book. The bulk of the acreage is in Ontonagon County, with the western border stretching into Gogebic County.

To study the whole park, you will need the following Michigan 15' quads: Carp River (covers the northeast section), White Pine (covers northwest section), Thomaston (covers southwest section), and Bergland (covers southeast section). The Carp River and White Pine quads cover the northern three-fifths of the park, where the climbing is done. Very little of the Bergland map is park land; for economy, this could be dispensed with. The only real climbing area in the park, the rugged basalt escarpment overlooking Lake of the Clouds, straddles the Carp River and White Pine maps, so both are necessary to study the topography.

State Highway 107 provides easy access to the Lake of the Clouds escarpment. From main highways that lead to the northern shore of the Upper Peninsula, take SH 107 west from Silver City and to the end of the road at Lake of the Clouds. Park maps show the area clearly.

One other road, SH 519, connects to 107 near Silver City. Highway 519 runs along the south boundary of the park and is used to reach Presque Isle.

CLIMBING

The Lake of the Clouds scenic overlook in Porcupine Mountains State Park is an ancient lava flow of amygdoloidal basalt, whose eroded end forms the cliff face. The escarpment to the northwest dips down toward Lake Superior. During what is known as the Keweenawan period, geologists believe lava poured out of the earth to form much of the surface of the Upper Peninsula. Only in the north have uplift and erosion been extensive enough to strip away all the younger rock to bare the oldest pre-Cambrian rock.

The Lake of the Clouds escarpment at Porcupine Mountains State Park. *(Minnesota Dept. Economic Development)*

The Lake of the Clouds escarpment, so known because it overlooks scenic Lake of the Clouds two hundred feet below, is an apparently little known climbing area. Few people are either willing to make the long drive to the park from the more populous centers of the Midwest, or they just don't know that climbing exists there, since few people scale the rocks. The cliff, however, is at least three hundred feet of excellent rock wall, with cracks and slabs similar to the basalt-formed north shore of Minnesota above Duluth, and is very accessible to climbers.

Some of the molten rocks of the lava flows that created the Upper Peninsula also formed the area north of Duluth. When the magma there failed to reach the earth's surface, it solidified slowly to create a gabbro several thousand feet thick. This gabbro is now exposed in the form of huge rock slabs that line the shores of Lake Superior for many miles.

Harder than sandstone, this lava type rock is excellent for climbing because it is very solid. The little climbing that is done in the Porcupines is carried out in the middle section of the ridge, the section of the escarpment that is nearest the west end of the lake. Just drive to the Lake of the Clouds overlook on SH 107 (park road) and park in the lot provided. You can't miss it.

Climbers can use the whole ridge (moving east from the lake would be best). The ridge runs for about three miles along the shore of Lake Superior.

Norwich Ledge

A similar formation in the general vicinity of the Lake of the Clouds escarpment is an area not shown even on most forest maps. A retired conservation officer told me of it and said that many local people don't even know it exists. It is an ideal spot for climbers with a strong urge for discovering new areas.

East of the Porkies is the Norwich Ledge. A five-mile long volcanic (basalt) rock cliff abuts the west branch of the Ontonagon River and forms an excellent climbing site. A topographic map (Matchwood 15′ USGS quadrangle) would be very helpful in locating the area precisely.

Unknown to climbers until now, the two to three hundred-foot high cliffs are worth the extra effort to find. The rock is part of the old Norwich mine range that runs east to Victoria and Rockland. To get to

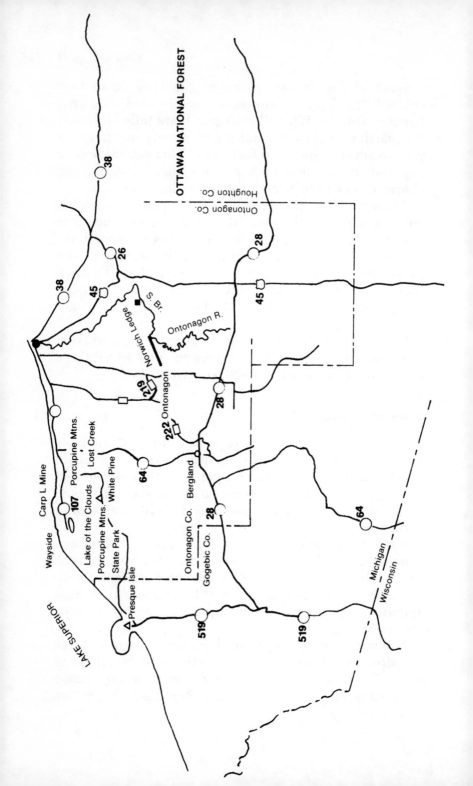

Norwich Ledge from Porcupine Mountains State Park, follow SH 64 east through Silver City and the town of Green. Turn right (south) on 64 (where it turns to go back toward White Pine). A few miles down the road bear left (due south) on FR 219 and follow it until it turns east and joins FR 178. At the junction, turn left on 178 (going north away from the Norwich mine). Drive about a half-mile north until you can turn right (east) again and proceed east on this road (FR 219) about four miles. (It is eight miles more to Rockland.) Park along the road and bushwhack through the woods about a half-mile south, until you come to the escarpment (about half way to the river). You can't miss it if you follow a 180° compass bearing.

There are no trails in the woods other than deer paths, so it is tough going through the dense vegetation. But when you reach the ledge, you'll find solid basalt walls almost three hundred feet high, with a variety of good climbing surfaces. There are some breaks in the wall where you can climb to the bottom without having to rappel. It might be best to climb down to examine the rock before beginning a rappel.

ACCOMMODATIONS AND OTHER ATTRACTIONS

Two modern and three rustic camp grounds in Porcupine Mountains State Park provide a total of 183 improved and 19 unimproved camp sites within the park boundaries. The modern camp grounds, Presque Isle River on the west and Union Bay on the east side of the park, are nearly always full, but three other camp grounds, referred to as outpost sites, are usually available. These outpost areas are Union River Campground with three sites, White Pine Extension Campground with eight sites, and Lost Creek Campground with five sites. Hot showers, flush toilets, electricity, and sanitation stations are available at Union Bay. Sites at Presque Isle River have no electricity.

Trailside camping is permitted, but not within a quarter mile of any cabin or Adirondack shelter developed for trail hikers. Sites are available on a first-come, first-serve basis and may not be reserved in advance. The only facilities offered in Adirondack shelters are bunks. Campfires for cooking are permitted in the interior of the park unless extremely dry conditions prevail, but no fires are allowed within shelters. Backpackers must register at the park office before entering the interior of the park. Disposable metal and glass containers are not to be taken into the park's interior.

Trailside cabins are available for rent from April 1 through November 30. These units are accessible only by foot and must be reserved in advance. One eight-bunk cabin is located at Mirror Lake. The remainder contain four bunks. Rental rates are about $10 per night per cabin.

The cabins include bunks with springs, mattresses, wood stoves, sink, cupboard, table and benches, cooking utensils, dishes, tableware, saw, and axe. Cabin users should provide bedding, food, towels, lighting, and personal items. Rowboats are furnished at Mirror Lake, Lily Pond, and Lake of the Clouds cabin at no extra charge.

Reservations for cabins should be made in advance with the park supervisor. Advance reservations are not considered until January 1 of the calendar year. The maximum length of stay in the Lake of the Clouds cabin is three days; all others are seven days. The cabins rent from noon to noon. A deposit of the total rent should accompany all reservations. Keys are issued at the park office.

Two small parks near the town of Bergland offer additional camp sites. Bergland Township Campground, in town on SH 28, has 12 camp sites. It is open May through September. Ontonagon County Park, on CR 64, has 30 sites and is open all year.

Motels are available in Ontonagon and Bergland and information is available at the Ontonagon Chamber of Commerce at (906) 884-4735.

A number of scenic trails in the park are Lake Superior Trail, at sixteen miles the longest in the park, follows rugged shoreline affording outstanding views. Pinkerton Trail, three miles, crosses Pinkerton Creek which has fine brook trout in various sections. Little Carp River Trail, eleven miles, winds past scenic waterfalls. North Mirror Lake Trail, four miles, cuts through the heart of the Porkies, ending at Mirror Lake, 1,531 feet high—the highest lake in Michigan—with good fishing for lake, brook, and rainbow trout. Union Mine Trail, a one-mile, interpretive trail, leads to ruins of an old copper mine.

Grand Ledge

DESCRIPTION

Some good, solid sandstone bluffs and the more urban environment at Grand Ledge, near Lansing, produce a completely different climbing atmosphere than is found in the wilderness area of the Upper Peninsula. At Grand Ledge, two city parks with a combined sixty acres contain the climb sites, each on opposite sides of the Grand River, from which the town derives its name. Park trails lead to climb sites on both sides of the river.

The bigger (fifty acres) park is Fitzgerald Park, off Jefferson Street in the city of Grand Ledge. Jefferson Street connects with SH 43. The smaller park (ten acres), Oak Park, is at the end of West Front Street, on the northwest end of town.

LOCATION

Grand Ledge, located approximately ten miles west of Lansing, sits on the intersection of SH 100 and SH 43,

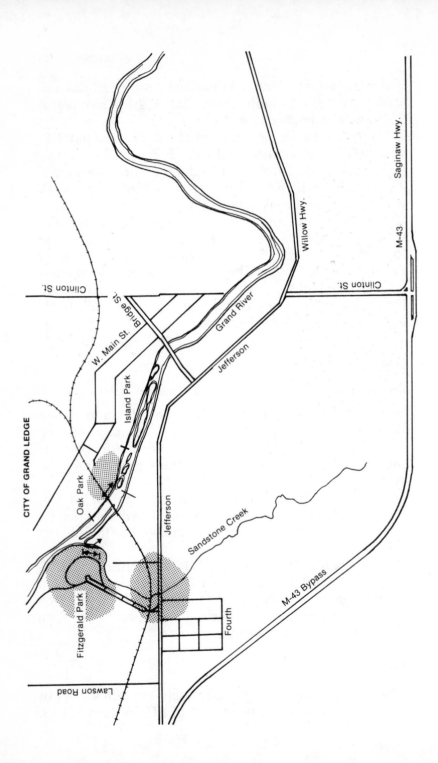

CITY OF GRAND LEDGE

Clinton St.

W. Main St.

Bridge St.

Island Park

Oak Park

Fitzgerald Park

Lawson Road

Jefferson

Sandstone Creek

Fourth

Jefferson

Grand River

Clinton St.

Willow Hwy.

M-43

Saginaw Hwy.

M-43 Bypass

about four miles south of Interstate 96, in Eaton
County. The Portland (Michigan) USGS 15′ quad
shows the Grand Ledge climbing areas. The climbing
areas are so small that it is easy to find your way
around the two parks.

CLIMBING

At the east side of Fitzgerald Park are stairs down the
cliffs. A little bridge crossing Sandstone Creek leads to
a number of small paths you can walk up and down to
the climb sites along the river. The ledges basically
follow the river and extend roughly to the area of the
three islands east of the train trestle. The paths continue to a section of the park known as "the carvings,"
where some of the climbing is done. The carvings
consist of pictures, names, and dates going as far back
as the seventeenth century. There is only a small
amount of rappelling done on this side of the river,
since climbers are attempting to preserve the rocks
containing the historic carvings. Most of the climbing
is done on the Oak Park side.

Oak Park, while smaller than Fitzgerald, is better
suited for climbing. Here, twenty to seventy-foot high
sheer ledges along the river extend from the train
trestle for approximately three-fourths of a mile north
and about one mile south. Rappelling is a favorite
climbing activity at Oak Park. The cliffs have good
climbing routes and easy access because of a number
of connecting foot paths.

The size and crackless nature of the formation almost require the use of a top rope on most routes. Free
climbing, except on the Bolt Route or on chocks, is the
only acceptable way of scaling the very fragile rock.
The climbing is strenuous and difficult, with fewer
than ten routes rated F5 or lower. Small holds, face
climbing, and vertical and overhanging routes predom-

inate. The lack of adequate jam cracks and clean protection placements add to the difficulty, especially when attempting to lead.

During the past few years, a number of clean leads have been accomplished by area climbers. Some of the best climbs at Grand Ledge are Despondency and Intimidator, two of the most difficult and boldest there. Also try Building Blocks (F7), Jay's Overhang (F6), and Overextension (F5). Area climbers can point out these routes.

To get to Oak Park from Fitzgerald Park, take West Jefferson east to the main red light in Grand Ledge (South Bridge and West Jefferson streets). Turn north on Bridge and continue across the river. Take the first street on your left (West Front) to the park. The ledges are on the west side of the river.

ACCOMMODATIONS AND OTHER ATTRACTIONS

Camping around Grand Ledge is not the greatest. Well-maintained rustic camp grounds that climbers might prefer are nonexistent and modern facilities are a bit impersonal. Nonetheless, the Lansing KOA, a private camp ground off I-96 at Business Route 96 (Cedar Street) and Aurelius Road, offers nearly all the comforts of home, from May through October. The 112 modern sites have full hookups, showers, swimming pool, laundry, and store, offering an economical alternative to a motel.

Motels are available in Lansing and East Lansing, as well as in some of the surrounding towns and cities.

Climbing Areas: Minnesota
  Carlton Peak
  Shovel Point
  Palisade Head
  Interstate Park (Minnesota/Wisconsin)

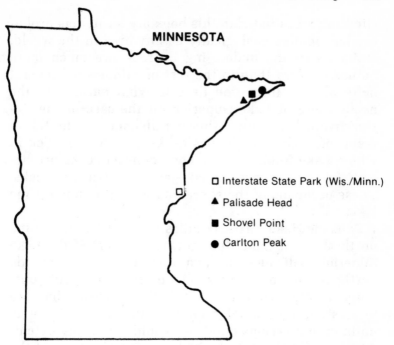

MINNESOTA

□ Interstate State Park (Wis./Minn.)
▲ Palisade Head
■ Shovel Point
● Carlton Peak

Four great glaciers advanced and retreated over Minnesota, gouging, planing, and rearranging the land, their signatures written clearly in the rocky, bluff-bound shores of Lake Superior and elsewhere throughout the state. When the ice finally melted, the face of the land looked much as it does today.

While a large part of Minnesota's surface is level or gently rolling, some areas, like the North Shore in the northeastern section of the Arrowhead region, stand out in bold relief. Here on Lake Superior's north shore, a very large mass of submerged lava flow, several thousand feet thick, crops out at the vicinity of Duluth, where it has been exposed by erosion. This mass, called the Duluth Gabbro, was the result of extensive Keweenawan igneous activity.

The northeastern part of Minnesota, where three

climbing areas listed in this book are located, is probably as complex geologically as any area in the world. Outcrops of the underlying bedrock are much more numerous here than in the rest of Minnesota. Several belts of rock formation lie somewhat parallel to the north shore of Lake Superior. In the case of the Keweenawan lava flows, this parallelism is definitely a result of erosion of the basin-like structure of rock in which Lake Superior lies. The youngest rocks are basalt flows and associated gabbro intrusive rocks. These occur along the shore and are tilted toward the lake.

Palisade Head, fifty-six miles north of Duluth on the north shore of Lake Superior, is the start of the Lake Superior palisades, a lava rock base that extends northeast for forty miles. There are some scenic outcrops located southwest of Palisade Head that are interesting individual rock formations, but there is nothing that serious climbers would use to any extent. At Silver Creek Cliff, the highway is carved out of the side of the sheer precipice, affording an inspiring view of Lake Superior and the rugged, rocky shore, but nothing in the way of climbing.

A little farther north along the shore, at Gooseberry Falls State Park, the picturesque Gooseberry River flows swiftly from the upland down the steep slope to Lake Superior. Igneous rock outcroppings are common in the park, dotted through by a second-growth forest of birch, poplar, alder, and black spruce. The river enters the park at a height of 240 feet, cascades over two waterfalls, and splashes under the highway bridge that crosses the gorge just below the first falls.

Farther north along U.S. Route 61 is Split Rock Lighthouse. It stands a hundred feet above the water on a particularly bold diabase cliff. Masses of white intrusive rock, called anorthosite, occur at many places from Split Rock north to Carlton Peak. They all appear to be huge fragments from underground that have been brought up by molten material when the diabase was formed. The anorthosite is resistant to erosion and the layer masses stand up as prominent rounded hills.

At Palisade Head, east of Beaver Bay, the Great Palisades form one of the most prominent features of the Minnesota shoreline. The palisade is composed of a dense, reddish, porphyritic felsite lava. The top of the palisade is very soft and easily eroded by waves, which leave horizontal crevices in the face of the cliff.

About two miles northeast of the Great Palisades are the Little Palisades. They are formed of the same kind of porphyritic felsite, but the presence of jointing, or fracturing, of the rock into vertical columns allows the wave erosion to keep a vertical cliff here. Because of this fracturing, a series of six-sided columns are present along the body of the cliff.

From this point northward for many miles, the land is quite level until Tofte, where Carlton Peak, a huge dome of hard anorthosite feldspar, rises to 1,529 feet above sea level. The tough anorthosite has resisted erosion, causing the hill to stand high above the softer lava flows along the shore. Just back of the shore in western Cook County is a series of ridges with serrate tops that can be seen from Carlton Peak. The ridges are called the Sawtooth Mountains and were formed by the unequal erosion of alternating hard and soft layers of rocks, all of which dip toward Lake Superior. Sawtooth topography occurs at many places in Cook County, but the term truly refers to the hills west of Grand Marais.

Carlton Peak

DESCRIPTION

Carlton Peak, near Tofte in Cook County, is the highest peak on the north shore, 927 feet above Lake

Superior. It is the region's most popular climbing area because it contains a variety of easy and hard climbs.

LOCATION

Found on the Tofte (Minnesota) 7½' USGS quad, the rugged hill is a few miles inland from the town of Tofte on the Sawbill Trail, a dirt road that leads to the interior wilderness area.

Take the Sawbill Trail west for about four and one-half miles and turn onto the Tofte dump road. Take the dump road about two miles past the dump and drive as far as is practical. The dirt road is sometimes washed out. If so, merely park where you can and hike to the peak. The road leads directly to the bottom of the hill.

CLIMBING

The climbing on Carlton Peak is fairly well known. On many weekends twenty to thirty people climb the two dozen or so routes ranging in difficulty from classes 3 and 4 to some F10+ tricky overhangs. The rock is not too exposed, as is the case with Palisade Head. Many more climbers work out here than at Palisade.

The climbs begin where the access road ends. A few yards' hike over some boulders puts you on the south and west sides of the hill (the ones you can see from the road).

Cracks for leading and faces for top roping make up the two types of climbs that predominate at Carlton Peak. Top roping is the standard here, but a few climbers lead with chocks. The rock faces are generally not as steep as Palisade Head.

ACCOMMODATIONS and OTHER ATTRACTIONS

See Shovel Point Accommodations.

Shovel Point. *(Alan Bagg)*

Shovel Point

DESCRIPTION

Shovel point is a 170-foot wall of sheer-face rock overlooking Lake Superior, part of Baptism River State Park, thirty-three miles northeast of Two Harbors. The park, established because of its outstanding scenic beauty, is just south of the hilly area known as the Sawtooth Mountains. There are no campsites or picnic grounds here, but there are a number of hiking trails that lead to good climbing. Two miles of wooded hiking trails lead the interested climber to the bluffs overlooking Lake Superior.

The Baptism River flows rapidly and noisily through the park. Lined by thick timber on both sides of the gorge and at the river mouth, the water surges over the highest waterfalls in the state, as well as several smaller ones.

East of the mouth of the Baptism River, rock outcrops are continuous along the lake shore. There are eleven or twelve lava flows along the shore between the river and the thick red flow that forms the Little Palisades, known as Shovel Point. Here SH 61 turns inland some distance to avoid the extremely rough Shovel Point coast.

Three miles northeast of the Baptism River, the highway swings around a large hill that consists principally of anorthosite. Beyond the hill, the rugged topography ends and the country slopes back gently to the upland for about eight miles to the Manitou River.

Location

Shovel Point is located off U.S. Route 61, about one mile south of the junction of SH 1. The climbing area is reached by parking in the lot provided off Rt. 61. To reach the climb sites, follow the trail to the lake. Both the Shovel Point and Palisade Head areas are located on the Illgen City (Minnesota) 7½' USGS quad.

Climbing

The trail to the climb sites goes northeast from the parking lot. Follow the route until you can scramble to the bottom of the rocks or find a suitable anchor at the top from which to rope down. You'll find a number of climbs in the general vicinity of Shovel Point, but some of the better ones have been cleaned of loose rock and "claimed" by the Outward Bound School, who uses the Shovel Point area as a practice climb site for its outdoor-education programs. Small groups of the well-supervised climbers are often there to learn on Saturdays. This area is more secluded than the better-known Palisade Head and farther southwest of Shovel Point, near Silver Bay.

The climbs at Shovel Point vary in difficulty, depending on the degree of vertical pitch. Many of the routes start on a ledge that runs midway between the top of the cliff and the waters of Lake Superior below. At many points (farthest east), there is no level shoreline on which to begin a climb. Instead, climbers here rappel to a ledge and begin their climbing from there. At the southernmost climbs, the routes are not challenging enough from the rocky shore and must be started higher. The Shovel Point climbs are fairly difficult, just as they are at Palisade Head, ranging generally upwards of 5.6. The cliffs reach 150 feet in height in most places, so a one-rope pitch is about the right length of climb. Most climbs are top roped, since it is difficult to find adequate protection midway down the cliff to set up a belay.

Exploration is important here, because no guidebooks are available on North Shore climbing sites.

The climbs at Shovel Point vary in difficulty, depending on the degree of vertical pitch. *(Alan Bagg)*

Climbers should be prepared to do a good bit of rock studying, both while climbing and while scouting out the climbs, both for safety and to insure pleasurable climbing. There are numerous places where a 150-foot rope won't reach the bottom of a rappel, so be careful you know what's at the bottom.

Feel free to explore the rock but in doing so, climbers should remember that this area is still unspoiled and the northern range is a delicate area, with an ecosystem that won't tolerate abuse either through overuse of the trail system, trampling down the fragile plant life, or littering the landscape. The extremely popular Boundary Waters Canoe Area (BWCA) is located just to the north of Silver Bay, and the number of persons that can enter the area is now limited by governmental control. Written permits are required to use the BWCA. Similar restrictions can be placed on climbers if care is not taken to preserve what is available today.

ACCOMMODATIONS AND OTHER ATTRACTIONS

Private accommodations near Shovel Point include Whispering Pines Motel in Silver Bay, and Colonial Inn, Manitou Falls Resort, and Ben Fenstad Resort in Little Marais. Camping includes Manitou Falls Campground and cabins include Colonial Inn, Art's Cabins, Fenstal's Resort, and Manitou Falls Resort. They are given more detail in a free flyer from the North Shore Tourist Association (also see accommodations listed under Palisade Head).

Baptism River State Park is an undeveloped wayside park with no facilites, running water, or buildings. There is no fee charged to use the grounds.

The hiking trails lead to some very beautiful sights near Shovel Point. The trail that goes southwest from the parking lot follows the Baptism River upstream, across the highway, and along the upper bank, a mile

Climbers should be prepared to do a good bit of studying the rock both while climbing and while scouting out the climbs at Shovel Point. *(Alan Bagg)*

and one half to the upper falls. The high falls are spectacular and offer ice-climbing possibilities in winter.

Palisade Head

DESCRIPTION

Palisade Head is a large cliff area, part of the Great Palisades in Lake County, two miles north of the town of Silver Bay on U.S. Route 61.

While no guidebook describes the individual routes that have been put up here, the area is a popular tourist attraction and well known to climbers in Minnesota. Yet it is not heavily climbed like Carlton Peak to the north or Taylors Falls to the south, near St.

Palisade Head is a favorite spot where tourists can watch climbers scaling the 200-foot sheer cliffs. *(Alan Bagg)*

Paul, where droves of university students flock to the park every weekend. The main reason Palisade Head is not more popular is that in terms of difficulty, it is more than the ability of many climbers. There are still some possible routes that haven't been climbed.

The park has no facilities, so everything you bring in must be taken out. There aren't even outhouses on the premises or garbage cans, thanks to local vandals who seem to delight in throwing them over the cliff. Managed as a state highway wayside park and marked as such, the state allows no camping since there are no facilities. It is simply a day-use area only.

LOCATION

From Highway 61, follow the road signs to Palisade Head. Park in the paved-and-gravel loop provided for vehicles and walk a few yards to the ledge at the climb site. A topographic map is hardly necessary, but in case one should be desired, order the Illgen City 7½′ (Minnesota) for best detail and the Finland (Minnesota) 15′ quad for the best overall picture of the surrounding terrain.

CLIMBING

The climbing at Palisade Head is difficult because of the sheer faces, extreme exposure and long crack systems, tight chimneys, and small handholds on the faces. Be prepared for many 5.7 (and harder) climbs on the basalt rock. There are only three existing routes easier than 5.6 at Palisade Head. A good number of 10s or harder and some strenuous crack climbs of the F8-F9 variety are ample tests of your ability.

Climbing access is from the top because the road leads to the top of the bluff. Climbers who desire to start at the bottom can walk to the south and find

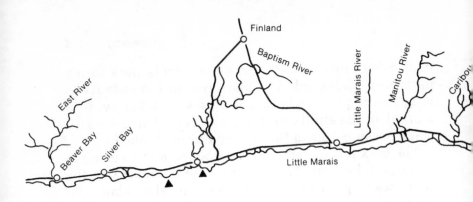

Finland
Baptism River
East River
Beaver Bay
Silver Bay
Little Marais River
Manitou River
Caribou
Little Marais

▲ Climb site

some Class 4 trails down to the bottom, about two hundred yards south of the parking area. Most climbers simply rappel to the bottom and begin searching for routes from the shoreline. There is a fairly substantial rocky beach area below the cliffs. If you hike down, look for a permanent safety rope near two gullies. Descend there using the rope provided. Since the cliff is sheer and is not cabled, roped, or fenced off, the area is fairly dangerous for non-climbers. Many tourists come to watch climbers dangling from prussik slings on the side of the rock.

The climbs at Palisade can be lead on nuts or top roped, but because no books detail the routes, leaders must be good at sizing up new routes or be able to explore the rock as they climb. When looking for routes here, it is often necessary to carefully scrutinize a hundred yards of rock in either direction, left or right.

Most of the roped pitches at Palisades are fifty to sixty feet, but there are a good number of them where a 150-foot rope won't reach the bottom of the cliff, so be sure you know what's at the bottom.

There are some good spots to rappel where half the drop is free hanging. (The tourists really turn on to

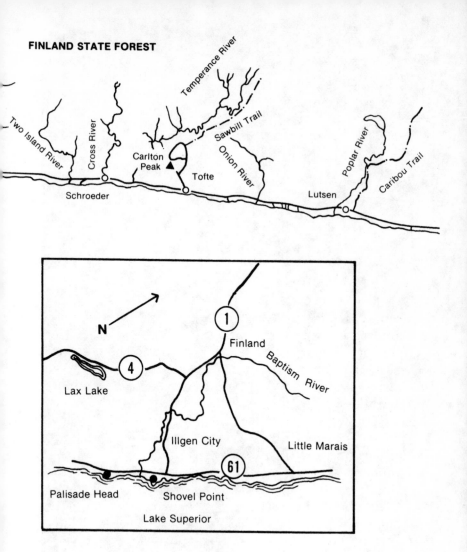

that.) There also are some two-hundred-foot cliffs in the immediate vicinity.

ACCOMMODATIONS AND OTHER ATTRACTIONS

Both camping and motels are not as abundant as you might expect in this "tourist"-type region. The variety of accommodations is not very great either. Prices are generally high as one would expect; quality is gener-

Climber's view of Palisade Head. *(Minnesota Dept. of Economic Development)*

Rappelling is the easiest way to get down to the beginning of the climb at Palisade Head. *(Alan Bagg)*

ally lower than might be expected. Both the motels and camp grounds seem to be rustic and a bit on the shabby side.

A number of state parks offer camping for a fee plus park admission, which is no more economical than private camp grounds but provides much more scenic surroundings as a rule. Gooseberry Falls, the second most visited park in Minnesota, has a campground, as does Crosby-Manitou, Manitou Falls, and Temperance River state parks.

The following private facilities, all located on U.S. 61, are available for camping: Linden's Cabins and Camping in Two Harbors, and Castle Haven Resort and Palisade Inn and Campgrounds in Silver Bay. Linden's also has cabins. Other cabin accommodations include Dean's Cabins, Twin Points Resort, Gooseberry Cabins, and Split Rock Cabins, all in Two Harbors.

Motels include Valhalla and Twin Points in Two Harbors, Spruce Point in Beaver Bay, and Mariner and Palisade Inn and Palisade Motel in Silver Bay.

Interstate State Park (Minnesota/Wisconsin)

DESCRIPTION

As its name suggests, Interstate Park is jointly operated by Minnesota and Wisconsin. This unusual
arrangement was Wisconsin's first venture into a state
park. Established in 1900, Interstate is the oldest in
the system which today numbers more than fifty
parks.

The two-state park spans the St. Croix River, the
border between the states. In this area, the river has
cut deeply into rocks formed from lava that welled up
in this area from the earth's molten center. The combined effects of the river's erosive quality and glacial
meltwaters have produced a spectacular and striking
scenic area at this point, widely known as the Dalles
of the St. Croix. The narrow gorge takes its name from
the French term *dalles*, meaning a narrow, rock-bound
river channel.

The St. Croix River gorge is one of the most scenic
areas in the state. Vertical cliffs as high as one
hundred feet occur along the river, and the rock outcrops extend up the valley wall more than three
hundred feet above the river. These rocks are old
Keweenawan basalt lava flows, of the same age as
those found on the shores of Lake Superior, from Duluth to Grand Portage, and on Keweenaw Point on the
Upper Michigan shore.

A striking feature of the gorge is the plane surfaces
of the cliffs. These are a result of the rock falling away
along fractures. Here, two hundred feet above the
roaring river below, are unusual rock formations, including the most striking, the Old Man of the Dalles, a
clearly sculpted profile. Other awesome rock formations abound, including potholes drilled into the rock
by rushing waters. These huge potholes are perhaps
the greatest curiosity of the region; there are eighty of

Rocks can be climbed on both sides of the St. Croix River in Interstate Park. *(Alan Bagg)*

them exposed on the flat surface of the lava flows on the Minnesota side of the river, located between the interstate bridge and the boat landing.

These potholes are cistern-like holes varying in size from foot-wide depressions to huge wells. The so-called Glacier Kettle is 60 feet deep, 12 feet in diameter at the surface, 15 feet in diameter at the 42-foot depth, and only 13 feet wide at the bottom. All of the potholes were formed by eddies in the river's rapids where the swirl of water was strong enough to rotate sand and pebbles caught in slight depressions in the rock.

Downstream, beyond the Dalles, the rocky bluffs flanking the valley are composed of marine sedimentary rocks of Cambrian and Ordovician age.

There are three prominent climb sites on the Wisconsin side: the Old Man area, the River Bluffs area, and Summit Rock. There is one large area on the Minnesota side, formed by the various rock outcrops along the trail.

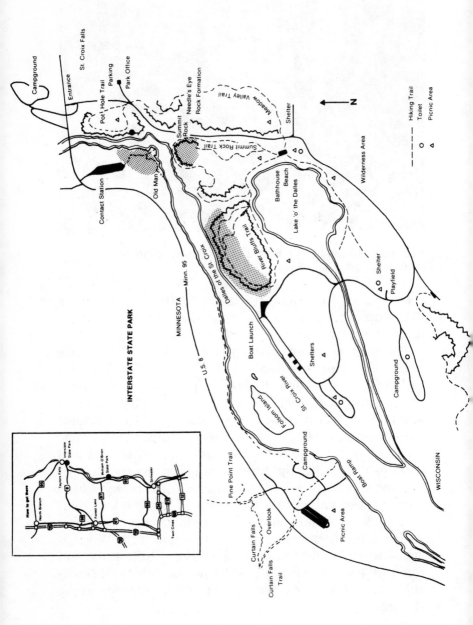

INTERSTATE STATE PARK

MINNESOTA

U.S. 8

Minn. 95

WISCONSIN

Campground
St. Croix Falls
Entrance
Pot' Hole Trail
Parking
Park Office
Contact Station
Old Man
Summit Rock
Needle's Eye
Rock Formation
Meadow Valley Trail
Summit Rock Trail
Bathhouse
Beach
Lake 'o' the Dalles
Shelter
Wilderness Area
River Bluffs Trail
Dalles of the St. Croix
Boat Launch
Shelters
Folsom Island
St. Croix River
Shelter
Playfield
Campground
Campground
Pine Point Trail
Curtain Falls Overlook
Curtain Falls Trail
Boat Ramp
Picnic Area

N

— — — Hiking Trail
O   Toilet
△   Picnic Area

How to get there
North Branch
Taylors Falls
Interstate State Park
William O'Brien State Park
Stillwater
Forest Lake
Twin Cities

LOCATION

Interstate Park is located near the towns of St. Croix Falls, Wisconsin, and Taylors Falls, Minnesota. The park straddles the St. Croix River and each park side has entrances on its respective bank of the river. The main entrance to the climbing areas on the Minnesota side is off Minnesota SH 95, just east of Taylors Falls. The Dalles of the St. Croix are located in the north section of the park. Another section to the south contains the campground and picnic areas. The shoreline is flat and without climb sites here.

The Wisconsin side of the park is entered from U.S. Route 8, just across the river from Taylors Falls, near St. Croix Falls. The camp ground area is north of highway 8. The main part of the park, including the two climbing areas, sits south of the highway.

The USGS topographic map quadrangle that covers this area is the St. Croix Dalles NW (Minnesota) 7½′.

CLIMBING

Rock climbing at Taylors Falls, as the area is commonly known to climbers in the Midwest, is a crowded affair most of the time. The routes in Interstate Park are well documented because of the heavy use by climbers throughout the year, particularly during the summer months.

A mimeographed guide booklet, "Climber's Guide to Taylors Falls," is available. The booklet, containing an excellent series of pictures, details the routes on the Minnesota and Wisconsin sides. Although very brief, the 8½ x 11-inch booklet is perhaps the best bargain of all the climbing guides, since it is sold at cost (plus postage if mailed) by the Midwest Mountaineering Shop, 309 Cedar Ave., Minneapolis, MN 55454 for about $1, postpaid.

As the climbing guide points out, the Dalles area can

Climbing at Taylor Falls involves many lava-formed slabs and faces. *(Alan Bagg)*

only be called modest in the size and scope of the climbs. None of them is more than eighty feet high, and many are more suited to bouldering than anything else. But there are a large number of climb routes that can be attempted. Fifty of the most popular ones are covered in the text and photos of the "Climber's Guide," but at least another fifty are not mentioned in the work. Some of the routes are extremely hard boulder problems that have attracted serious climbers who work on intricate moves on a short section of rock for the better part of a day. The most popular climbs are continually in use on summer weekends. Ninety percent of the routes are within close proximity to each other. The climbs lend themselves to top roping, but there are some excellent leads on both sides of the river, which should be done completely on nuts since the basalt is very solid.

On the Minnesota side, climbing sites are found along the Pothole Trail that leads to the rocky formations along the river. Park in the large main lot at the north entrance of the park. The presence of a concession stand and museum, in addition to many climbers carrying rope, lets you know you are in the right place. Follow the blacktop trail from the parking lot and you can't miss the climbs.

Devil's Chair is one of the most picturesque and prominent rock formations at the end of the trail leading along the river bank. This prominent rock pinna-

The Devil's Chair, on the Minnesota side of Interstate Park, is a spectacular rock formation. *(Alan Bagg)*

Crack climbing is an art practiced a great deal at Interstate Park.
(Alan Bagg)

cle, often pictured on postcards, contains an F9, five-inch flaring crack on the side facing the river. There are some tough free-climb pitches in the immediate vicinity.

The most interesting and advanced climbs are near the water's edge toward the end of the trail, past the excursion boat dock. One of the longest and most strenuous climbs at the Falls is the Piece of Cake route up the face of the prominent cliff you can see as you emerge from the trees just downriver from the boat dock.

There are also climbs to the north of the boat dock along the path leading from the parking lot to the dock. They are somewhat easier and less popular than those on the river. A classic dihedral route known as Sonny and Juanita (F5) was supposedly first scaled by three *voyageurs* from Duluth (along with their canoe) in 1909.

The Boneyards is a good bouldering area located beneath a railing about fifty feet north of the climb known as The Real Thing (toward the interstate bridge). You are in the right spot if you can locate a footbridge above you. The principal bouldering area is south of this footbrige.

On the Wisconsin side, a good number of interesting climbs can be reached by driving directly to the park or by walking across the interstate bridge from the Minnesota side. From the bridge, take the footpath by the river about three-eighths of a mile to the conspicuous sinkhole located near the first parking lot south of the bridge. A trail leads from this parking lot through the woods and a picnic area to the river. You will come out near a spot known as Impossible Crack. Getting down to the start of the climb is no easy task, but there is a relatively safe way (Class 4 and scramble) to walk down instead of rappelling. A gully marked only by a draw at the top of the rocks is the easiest way down, but it is not obvious or easy, to find the first time. The gully is to the right of Honeywell Project, one of the more popular climbs.

Some new climbs have been put up on Summit Rock, a rocky bluff between the park road and the river close to the Needle's Eye, a rock formation around which the road is built. Drive to the parking lot nearest Lake O' The Dalles and hike north on the Summit Rock Trail to the climb sites.

The Old Man formation and other climbs around the Pot Hole Trail are very popular, as are the climbing sites around Summit Rock. A valley separates the two areas, but the Summit Rock can be seen from the Old Man. The climbing at both areas is characterized by broken ledges of basalt, sixty to seventy feet high in the Potholes area and about one hundred fifty-foot high cliffs in the Summit Rock area.

Summit Rock climbs are mainly centered on the

northeast face. A trail leads to the bottom of the cliff and another leads to the top so climbers can choose whether to start from above or below. The cliff is roughly divided by ledges into three pitches of equal length, about fifty feet in height each.

There are a few climbs farther south along the River Bluffs Trail, but these are often hampered by high river water, which prohibits dropping to solid footing on the shoreline. When the river is low enough, some shoreline is exposed and climbs can be started from the bottoms of the cliffs. The pitches are in the seventy-five foot category at the Bluffs Trail.

While most of the climbs are done at the Potholes and Summit Rocks areas, the rock throughout the park is generally good and fairly solid for climbing, characterized by large cracks and some chimneys for chimney-climbing buffs.

ACCOMMODATIONS AND OTHER ATTRACTIONS

Included within the park boundaries on the Wisconsin side are camp grounds, picnic areas, hiking trails, scenic outlooks, and a small lake that provides a perfect swimming area. On the Minnesota side, many of the same features are present, and there is a commercial boat line that runs guided trips through the Dalles.

The river, of course, provides a focal point for the park, offering good fishing for many species. Canoeing through the Dalles is popular. The entire St. Croix River is now part of the National Scenic Riverway, not just the upstream portion.

The two camp grounds on either side of the park provide adequate camping facilities, but often they are completely filled by Friday night. On the Minnesota side there are 48 sites, 24 with electricity hookups, but no showers. The park is open all year except for limited service from December 1 to February 28.

Steep faces, although not extremely high, make the climbing on the moderate to hard side at Interstate Park. *(Scott Swanson)*

Camp Croix, a private camp ground on SH 243 near the town of Shafer, has 68 sites, many of them with full hookups and showers. Another private park in nearby Lindstrom is Whispering Bay, with 46 sites (showers) and a number of other facilities. It is open from May through October 15.

The Wisconsin side of Interstate Park has 95 rustic sites open most of the year. About fifteen miles northeast of St. Croix Falls on SH 35, the village park in Luck offers 25 sites open from April through September. Private camp grounds include Apple River Campground North, a wooded riverside park about twenty miles northeast of the state park. It contains 50 sites, some utilities, flush toilets, and hot showers, and is open all year. The Apple River is noted for its inner tubing on the rapids, a great diversion when it's too hot for climbing.

Country Dam Campsite, a small park (20 campsites) fourteen miles east of the park on U. S. 8, offers enroute overnight camping next to a restaurant with grassy open sites. You might consider this a possibility if all else fails on campsite hunting. Schillberg's Willow Lane Farm is a grassy, wooded, primitive camp ground with limited facilities near Osceola. It has a hundred sites and is open all year.

OHIO

Clifton Gorge:
John Bryan State Park

The Pleistocene glaciers planed Ohio nearly level except for the southeast, where narrow, forested valleys, steep hills, caves, and other striking rock formations prevail.

The tier of counties bordering Lake Erie was once under it. They are flat and rather swampy. A low divide separates the lake plain from the rest of the state, through which the most important streams flow to the Mississippi. The western half of this region is deep in glacial soil, while the rugged, rocky eastern portion is better suited to forestry. The topography of Ohio lends itself to climbing about the least of any of the Midwestern states. For this reason, the Clifton Gorge in John Bryan State Park, near Dayton, stands out like a rare gem. The scenic limestone gorge is part of the Little Miami River, which flows south to the Ohio River.

Geologists believe a widespread sea covered the section of land now known as John Bryan State Park, perhaps as many as 350,000,000 years ago. At this time sedimentary rocks beneath the surface—dolomites, shales, and limestone—were deposited or precipitated to the depth of several hundred feet. Later the land emerged from the sea and the most recently created rocks were slowly eroded by the steady, down-cutting waters of the present-day Little Miami River. After many years of constant erosion, Clifton Gorge came into existence, an attraction for Ohio's early settlers, not only for its beauty but also because the reliable stream provided the energy needed to run mills in the 1800s.

Designated a National Natural Landmark by the U.S. Department of the Interior, Clifton Gorge is perhaps the most outstanding example of an interglacial and postglacial canyon cutting into the dolomite of the Niagara escarpment in Ohio. In fact, no other area in Ohio can boast about as many remarkable natural features as the gorge area in northern Greene County.

About the only area on public property where serious climbing is permitted, John Bryan Park contains a number of cliffs that are popular to university students and others from the Dayton area, as well as from the rest of the state.

In addition to John Bryan State Park, the area containing many cliffs around Hocking Hills State Park, east of Chillicothe in southeast Ohio, allows a number of climbs on private property. Here, Blackhand quartzite sandstone layers of Mississipian age form up to two hundred-foot high bluffs in some places. Climbing is not allowed at Hocking Hills State Park, but by asking individual property owners you may be able to find some good climbing areas.

Similar in cliff-forming properties to the Hocking Hills area is the Sharon Conglomerate, a basal Pennsylvanian layer found in Jackson, Geauga, Portage, and Summit counties. Again, any climbing must be done by permission of individual land holders, which is usually a time-consuming and futile process.

Another possible climb area is in Adams County in southwest Ohio. Here cliffs of Silurian dolomite form many outcrops along streams and quarries that are primarily on private property. These are good for climbing.

Clifton Gorge (John Bryan State Park)

DESCRIPTION

Clifton Gorge is one of Ohio's most beautiful and unusual natural areas, preserved by Ohio's 1970 Natural Areas Act as a scientific and interpretive nature preserve. It is contained within boundaries of the John Bryan State Park, making up about a third of the park's eastern land area.

The form of the gorge is largely controlled by the massive Cedarville dolomite, a porous middle Silurian that forms bold, vertical cliffs and narrow gorges, and the more easily eroded and weathered Springfield dolomite, which outcrops near water level. The Little Miami River has cut through the overlying glacial material to the underlying rocks and at present is eroding through these formations, exposing them along the side of the gorge. However, most geologists believe that the gorge was cut largely during glacial times.

Evidence of glacial origin is provided by giant potholes, two to eight feet in diameter, found in the gorge and also on the rock ledges for some distance back from the gorge, particularly in the woods on the south side.

As the streams cut through the rocks, they encountered formations of varying resistance, sometimes with the softer rock below eroding faster to form an undercut. When the undercutting progressed far enough, the overhanging cliff toppled into the valley below, forming large slump blocks on the valley floor. Steamboat Rock is a fine example of such a slump rock. Farther downstream to the west in the area of the state park, the river has cut into lower, softer bedrock and the gorge widens out.

The abundant plant life and striking geological formations are what make this area so popular. The north side of the gorge is designated as an interpretive nature preserve, which allows public use. Because excessive public use would destroy or alter the plant communities, the south side of the gorge is restricted to scientific research and study, with access by written permit only. (Permits can be obtained from the Ohio Division of Natural Resources, Division of Natural Areas and Preserves.) Rock climbing is prohibited within the preserve, except in the areas designated by signs, and the use of pitons or other hardware that could ruin the rocks is strictly forbidden.

The 881-acre park was named after John Bryan, who donated his five hundred-acre Riverside Farm to the state in 1925. In 1950, the Ohio Division of Parks began managing the area. Since that time there have been other additions of land, bringing the park acreage to its present size.

LOCATION

The park is located in Greene County, near Clifton, on the Little Miami River. Entrance to the park can be made from SH 343 and SH 370, two miles east of

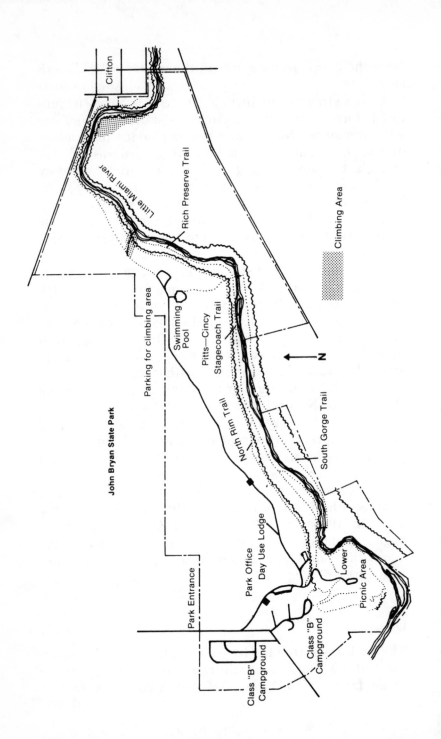

John Bryan State Park

Clifton

Little Miami River

Rich Preserve Trail

Parking for climbing area

Swimming Pool

Pitts—Cincy Stagecoach Trail

North Rim Trail

South Gorge Trail

Climbing Area

N

Park Entrance

Park Office Day Use Lodge

Class "B" Campground

Class "B" Campground

Lower

Picnic Area

Yellow Springs, ten miles south of Springfield, and twenty miles east of Dayton. The park office is located just off SH 370, approximately one mile from SH 343 and one city block from the park entrance on Park Road 1. Visitors may obtain park brochures and interpretive nature information at the office.

A sign at the entrance indicates the park. John Bryan State Park can be found on the Clifton (Ohio) 7½' USGS topographic quadrangle.

CLIMBING

Many climbers find this park a natural attraction because there is little else in the area and virtually nothing else in the state to climb on public property. Clifton Gorge attracts people from Kentucky and Indiana as well, because all public parks are closed to climbing in Indiana and stiff fines are handed out for violations. (Some climbers from this area go to the Red River Gorge near Slade, Kentucky, which has excellent limestone climbing.)

To reach the climbing sites at John Bryan, drive through the park and leave your car in the big lot northeast of the Orton swimming pool. Hike east along the Gorge Trail that rims the gorge on the north side of the river. Before the wall area, the trail splits and the left fork goes to the top, and the right heads toward the bottom. The lead climbs begin on the bottom. For top roping, take the trail to the left. There are many places to tie in on the top, but the area is very crowded with climbers on weekends—"swarmed" might be a better word. By 10 or 11 A.M. all the popular climb sites are full. Climbing classes use the park at least every month; much instruction by the area climbing clubs takes place there.

There is really only one area to climb near the northernmost bend in the river, not far from the Old

Inn ruins (marked on the state park maps). There are anywhere from fifty to seventy-five routes known by various names to the local climbing buffs, and usually on a good weekend there will be from seventy to a hundred people trying to climb them. Many of the climbers come from Ohio State University.

The pitches cover a range of difficulty from 5.1 to 5.9 and are found scattered along a half-mile section of river wall. There is usually a hundred-foot spit of land along the river bank on which you can stand to tie in and begin climbing or where you can drop to if you rappel. The limestone bluffs vary from forty to eighty feet in height.

There is no published climber's guide to the Clifton Gorge, but the University of Cincinnati Mountaineering Club has a single copy of a scrapbook type collection that describes some of the routes, including pictures, but they too have nothing printed on the subject.

ACCOMMODATIONS AND OTHER ATTRACTIONS

A 75-unit Class B camping area (and nearby group campsites) in the state park is available to climbers, but it is usually full on weekends. The sites are partially shaded and equipped with tables and grills; water and restrooms are located nearby. Open-field, group' campsites are available on a reservation-only basis, and reservations must be made at least fourteen days in advance through the park office. The address is Rt. 1, Box 74, Yellow Springs, OH 45387, (513)767-1274.

Other facilities at the park include a 45 x 120-foot swimming pool, picnic areas, a canoe launch for park guests, and a number of nature programs. Twelve hiking trails wind over ten miles of park terrain.

Buck Creek State Park, near Springfield, has day-use facilities only on its 4,030 acres. No camping is permitted there. Other camp grounds, in the area include 62 sites at Bass Lake Campground, 160 sites at Crawford Farm Market Campgrounds, and 50 sites at Gundolf's Recreation, near Springfield. All offer modern facilities, including showers and utilities. And there are 150 modern, improved sites at Enon Beach Campground, near Enon.

A number of interesting activities are possible when not climbing at Clifton Gorge. Named after Nathaniel Greene, the Revolutionary War period hero, Greene County is rich in historical significance. Five covered bridges still stand in the county, and Galloway Cabin is a reminder of pioneer days. The Glen Helen Natural Area, a rugged miniature wilderness, is part of the Antioch College campus, adjoining Yellow Springs. Rare wildflowers, ferns, and other moisture-loving plants grow here in this registered Natural Historic Landmark.

At Harveysburg, about twenty-five miles south of Clifton Gorge in Warren and Clinton counties, Caesar Creek State Park has a gorge preserve of about 460 acres. The gorge was created by volumes of glacial meltwater cutting down through the underlying bedrock. Gorge walls rise 180 feet above the valley floor and expose ordovician limestone and shale rich in fossils.

Waynesville, near Harveysburg, is a colonial town that offers one of the largest collections of antique shops in any Ohio community. There are about twenty shops in the village of approximately 1,800 people. A Sauerkraut Festival in October features German food, displays of cabbages, the judging of the largest cabbage, and plenty of sauerkraut.

Caesar's Creek Pioneer Village, recently developed and located north of Wellman on Clarksville Road, about twelve miles southeast of Waynesville, is a working pioneer settlement. There is a two-story 1807

house of beech logs on its original site, as well as five
buildings which were moved to the site and recon-
structed. Tours can be arranged.

Climbing Areas: Wisconsin (17 areas)
  Devil's Lake State Park (11 areas)
    Sandstone Area
    Guillotine Area
    East Bluffs Area
      Rainy Wednesday Tower
      The Leaning Tower
      The Four Brothers
      The Hawk's Nest
    Devil's Doorway
      Major Mass
      Minor Mass
    Balance Rock Area
    Railroad Tracks Area
    West Bluffs Area
  Gibraltar Rock (4 areas)
    Scotts Overhang Area
    Upper and Lower Roof Area
    Vertical Smile Area
    Danger Zone Area
  Abelman's Gorge (2 areas)
    Abandoned Quarry
    UW Plot

Glaciation is responsible for the face in Wisconsin, a
rolling plain broken in places by sharply uplifted
ridges of different geological composition. The ice
scraped and carved all but the rugged southwestern
quarter of the state, known as the Driftless Area.
Elsewhere, it created the nearly nine thousand lakes,
largest of which is Lake Winnebago. The glacier also
left moraines of valuable sand and gravel, kames,
eskers, and many other glacial phenomenon. A classic

WISCONSIN
- ■ Devil's Lake State Park
- ▲ Gibraltar Rock
- ● Abelman's Gorge
- △ Interstate State Park
  (see Minnesota)

example is the Kettle-Moraine area of southeastern Fond du Lac County.

The northern upland is the highest part of the state. The quartzite and drift hills of the Penokee Range are also in this region.

In the relatively flat central plain, cliffbound and beautiful Devil's Lake stands out in sharp relief. At the southern edge of this area, the quartzite Baraboo Range rises eight hundred feet above the plain. The lowest part of the state is the Lake Michigan shore.

Devil's Lake State Park

DESCRIPTION

Immersed in spectacular scenery, the sheer bluffs rising five hundred feet above Devil's Lake on three sides make the Devil's Lake State Park area the most popular and well-known climbing area in the Midwest.

Like a tremendous magnet drawing climbers from Illinois, Iowa, Minnesota, Michigan, and all parts of the eastern and western states, the quartzite bluffs provide some of the finest rock for climbing in the

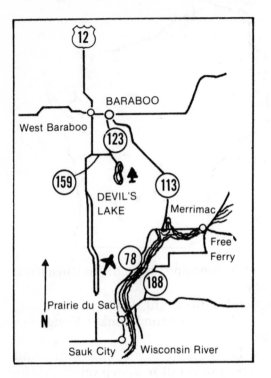

Midwest. Some western climbers have even claimed Devil's Lake to be the equal of some of America's finest climbing areas in the West, in terms of variety and difficulty.

Devil's Lake is an excellent training area since climbs here range in difficulty from easy enough for the beginner to very difficult (5.9 and aid-climbing pitches) challenges for even the most accomplished climbers. The climbing sites are all quite varied, yet accessible, and because of this, as well as the shortness of most pitches and their nearness to one another, one can quickly assimilate and practice rock climbing techniques here.

The six thousand acre park, run by the Wisconsin

Department of Natural Resources, is situated in one of the most scenic areas of Wisconsin, known as the Baraboo Range, a canoe-shaped range of hills approximately twenty-five miles long and ten miles wide, formed by the last glacier to occupy Wisconsin.

These ancient hills are composed of Baraboo quartzite, a unique rock consisting of tightly cemented grains of sand. The change from sandstone to quartzite involved little or no crushing of the sand grains; close examination of the rock reveals very distinguishable grains. Apparently, unlike the normal metamorphosis that takes place when heat and pressure interact, the transition from sandstone to quartzite was made solely by filling the spaces between the grains. When broken, the quartzite cracks through the sand grains, rather than around them as would happen when a piece of sandstone is broken. This condition contributes to the sharp-edged ledges characteristic of the Devil's Lake climbing area as opposed to the rounded holds of nearby sandstone areas. Except for the additional silica in the Baraboo quartzite, the composition of the rock is identical to that of many sandstones in southern Wisconsin. The reddish color of the quartzite is due to the presence of an extremely thin iron-oxide coating on most of the sand grains. Sometime after the glacial seas that deposited this sand withdrew, the quartzite was bent upwards and formed the Baraboo North and South ranges as we know them today.

Beyond the rock terrain inself, Devil's Lake State Park offers a tremendous amount of natural beauty, especially the vast variety of plant growth. Because of the variations in elevation, there are wide changes in climatic conditions. As a result, more than seven hundred species of ferns and flowering plants grow there.

Because of the park's topographic characteristics, it is divided into a north and a south section, with en-

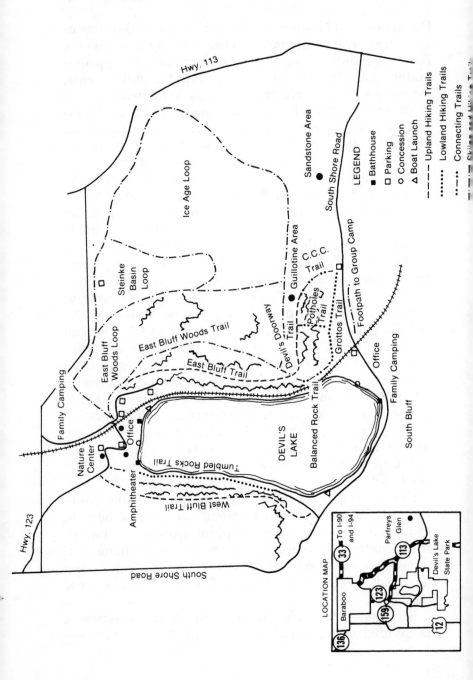

trances to either section provided from both the east and west. Each section has its own camping area, beach, bathhouse, picnic areas and shelters, concession stands, and boat launching areas. A park sticker, available at either park office, is required to use the park facilities. Camping fees are in addition to the daily or annual, resident or nonresident, sticker fees.

LOCATION

Easily spotted on any state highway map, Devil's Lake State Park is located three miles south of Baraboo and can be reached from SH 123 or from County Highway DL, which joins SH 113.

Climb sites are scattered throughout the park on the bluffs that ring Devil's Lake itself, the focal point of the park. Each of eleven climbing areas is described in more detail in the section that follows. The Baraboo (Wisconsin) 15′ quad covers part of the area. Another map, the North Freedom (Wisconsin) 15′ quad, covers the entire western portion of the Baraboo Hills. If you are in the area and need either map, they can be purchased at the U.S. Geological Survey office at 1815 University Avenue in Madison.

CLIMBING

There is an abundance of climb sites centered in a dozen main locations at Devil's Lake: the Sandstone area; Guillotine area, East Bluffs, including Rainy Wednesday Tower, Leaning Tower, Four Brothers, and Hawk's Nest; West Bluffs; Devil's Doorway areas; Balance Rock area; and teh Railroad Tracks area. All are easily accessible by well-marked and heavily traveled hiking trails.

With the virtual explosion of interest in climbing at Devil's Lake that began in the early 1970's it is little wonder that the rock structure has been mentally dissected and mapped, as a cadaver would be studied by a group of medical school students. As a result of this minute division after division of the major climbing areas, the hundreds of pitches throughout the park are known by a colorful assortment of names, the number of which stands it apart from all other climbing areas in the Midwest, and probably the entire United States.

An excellent guidebook, now out of print and difficult to find, gives many more detailed descriptions of the routes in each climbing area listed here than there is room for in this volume. While *Climbers and Hikers Guide to Devil's Lake*, edited by David Smith and Roger Zimmerman (published in 1970 by the Wisconsin Hoofer Mountaineers, University of Wisconsin at Madison) is out of print, a fair number of dog-eared copies, often photocopied from other photocopies, do show up along the trail.

The Sandstone Area

Approximately one mile east of the East Bluffs climbing area is a small section of sandstone cliffs. The cliff faces south and is on the same east-west ridge that contains Devil's Doorway and East Bluffs rocks. Although the area is not large, some of the climbs are almost ninety feet high, and the rock is of much better quality than typical southern Wisconsin sandstone. The area can be reached by hiking (or driving) two miles east from where the railroad tracks cross the road, running east from the South Shore Campground. The cliffs are visible about a quarter of a mile to the northeast on the hillside. There are a number of turnouts along the road in which to park a vehicle.

Among the numerous routes to climb, there are two recommended for their high quality. Curving Crack (F6), east of Morning Sickness, is a prominent crack that curves to the right at the top. This affords excellent practice at laybacking and jamming. The face just to the left is F9. To find Gargantua (F9) continue east from Curving Crack to a huge roof behind a large block of rock on the ground. This route, originally done with aid, has been led free. Surmount the roof, then follow the crack above to where it is capped by a large block. Hand traverse left and mantle to the top.

THE GUILLOTINE AREA

The Guillotine Area is a good place for beginning climbers because of the concentration of easy climbs. The area is divided into two levels: the lower level has the longest and most interesting climbs, the upper level rather short climbs and some interesting boulder problems. The base of the upper level is about one hundred fifty feet east of the Flatiron, a treacherous F10 boulder problem, recognized as the first prominent rock outcropping on the right side as you ascend the CCC Trail. The top of the lower climbs finish at this elevation.

The following listing of the more interesting climbs in this area includes a brief description of each. They are located by number on the accompanying map. Dots indicate other popularly climbed routes. Those dots with the letter "A" next to them indicate an aid climb.

LOWER GUILLOTINE AREA

1. The Little Thing (F4) is a good place for a beginner to practice a four-foot chimney. Climb up six feet to a shelf, then to the top using ledges and the chimney.

2. Annies's Overhang (F6) was named for a female climber who thought she had left her little finger in the jam crack. Many people since have experienced similar feelings. Ascend the crack and face four feet left of the

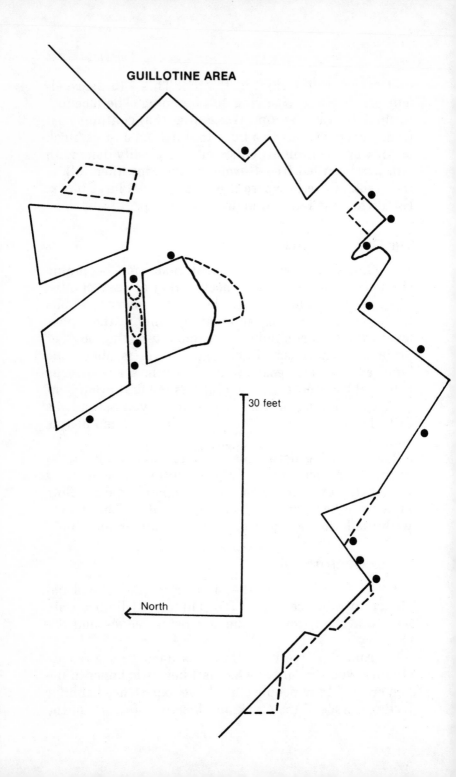

GUILLOTINE AREA

30 feet

← North

corner, fifteen feet to the bilevel roof. Use a good hand jam in the left crack above the roof and climb the right crack to the top.

3.   Beginner's Chimney (F4) should be climbed on the inside corner using chimney moves and ledges.

THE EAST BLUFFS

This fine climbing area is reached by hiking up the CCC Trail, which starts one mile east of the railroad tracks across from the old CCC camp, now part of the state park facilities. The more interesting climbs are:

1.   Sometime Crack (F9). Start at base of overhanging jamcrack in wall right of End (next entry). Ascend jamcrack to intersection A with horizontal crack. Traverse right five feet, and on to top. Sometine Crack, Right Side (F10). Ascend, if your body and mind are willing, to the upper limits of your ability. Start in thin cracks to the right of Sometime Crack to the traverse line above. Follow regular route up.

2.   The End (F9). Many zealous climbers have contemplated the nasty ground below and the overhanging nose above and cringed in terror at the realization of the total absence of piton cracks. Start on the overhanging nose, left of Sometime Crack, and climb nose to top.

3.   The Stretcher (F9). Only a series of bolts would permit a lead of this smooth face. Start on the smooth face ten feet right of Birch Tree Crack, then to the top.

4.   Upper Diagonal (F9) is a strenuous but well-protected climb. Use some discretion in deciding whether to fall above or below. Start the same as Birch Tree Crack. Climb up and left into diagonal crack, then follow crack to top.

Lower Diagonal (F8) offers experience in placing pitons on the run. Start the same as Birch Tree Crack. Climb the crack to ledge A, exit left to the upper section of the Pedestal.

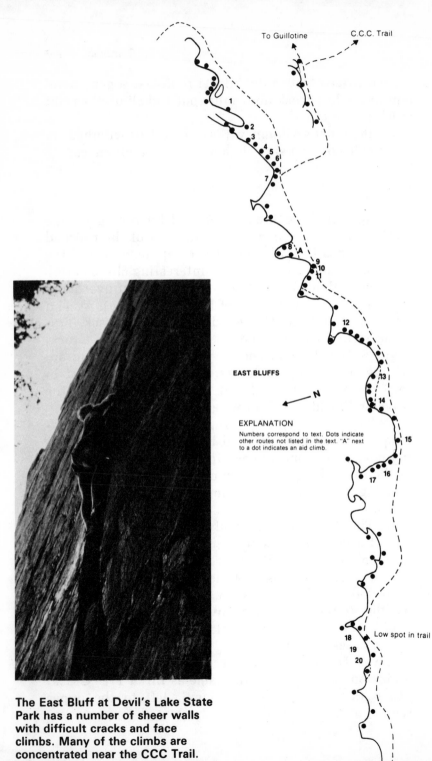

To Guillotine

C.C.C. Trail

1

2
3
4 5
6
7

8 A
9
10
11

12

EAST BLUFFS

← N

EXPLANATION

Numbers correspond to text. Dots indicate
other routes not listed in the text. "A" next
to a dot indicates an aid climb.

13

14

15

16
17

18

19

20

Low spot in trail

**The East Bluff at Devil's Lake State
Park has a number of sheer walls
with difficult cracks and face
climbs. Many of the climbs are
concentrated near the CCC Trail.**
(Alan Bagg)

5. The Pedestal (F5) is an interesting (classic) route, well worthwhile, multipitch lead. Start at the base of detached flake, right of corner. Climb flake to top, traverse left and up around corner to hidden belay ledge. Traverse left further to tree, then up crack above to ledge. Finish (although other finishes are possible and practical) by traversing right and up to top.

6. Condolences (F7). Start at the corner left of the Pedestal. Climb up and to the right to the left side of the flake on the Pedestal, layback up side of flake, then directly up wall above to ledge (follow corner closely).

7. Congratulations Crack (F9), one of the classic "hard" routes, is the scene of many leader falls. Start in the steep crack, ten feet to the left of Condolences. Climb crack to tree (same as on the Pedestal), then follow the Pedestal to the top.

8. Gill's Crack (F9). Start from Boy Scout Slab (halfway up). Climb crack to the top.

9. Brinton's Crack (F6) is a classic climb. It was first ascended in 1941, yet it still embarasses many climbers. A series of continuous, exposed moves makes this climb worthwhile for everybody. Start in crack in left side of face (buttress), beginning twenty feet up. Climb to rectangular alcove, traverse right to a prominent platform (Hilton Ledge), then up the crack (crux) to the top.

10. Brinton's Direct (F8). Do not traverse—continue directly to the top.

11. Berkeley (F6) is another classic climb. Try the regular route or, if more ambitious, the interesting variations. Start twenty-five feet left of corner, a prominent crack. Climb crack (passing a series of blocks) fifteen feet, then traverse right to alcove (A), continue on to a stance above (zig-zag right and left to clear bulge), then left and up to broken rock ("hanging chimney") and the top.

12. Vacillation (F7). Two decidedly interesting

moves make this climb worthwhile, yet a series of loose blocks provide for much indecisiveness. Start ten feet left of the Grotto in a crack. Ascend crack until below a square (slightly loose) block. Continue directly upwards to a bulge. The prominent crack above is climbed to the top.

13. Moderation (F4). Start at the broken rock left of Schizophrenia, then traverse right to a relatively easy corner, then follow corner to the top.

14. Anemia (F4) will yield to any technique, even *no* technique. (It is more interesting during the winter after a severe icing.) Start in inside corner (broken rock) on the right side of the face. Three pine trees are easily discerned above. Go up the corner, traverse left along a prominent ledge to a pine tree, then up and right, passing two more trees, to the top. (Numerous variations are possible above ledge.)

15. Peter's Project (F7) is a superb climb, both interesting and stimulating (from top to bottom and the other way around). Start in the prominent overhanging crack to the left side of the buttress, ten feet right of nose at Ostentation. Climb overhanging crack until the angle abruptly eases, then straight up to the base of a short wall. Climb wall (left of the more broken rock of Anemia) to a ledge, then up the small face (crux) to the top. (Try not to traverse off this elegant route.) Peter's Project Right Side (F9). Start by ascending face of right of Peter's Project. The crack is not used.

16. Michael's Project (F7). The crux is just above the ground. Start in prominent crack just left of Callipigeanous Crack. Climb up the crack, swing right, then up, then back into the crack. Exit right, then up to the top (same finish as Peter's Project).

17. The Black Rib (F10). The first crux is getting off the ground. Start on a blank wall, ten feet to the left of Michael's Project. Go to the "hanging" chimney above.

18. The Cheatah (F9) has exceptionally continuous

routes. Avoid the small tree on the delicate mantle halfway up. Start thiry feet right of Push-Mi Pull-Yu. Climb up to crack, up the crack system past a small tree to a difficult (indeed, decidedly unpleasant) lay-back problem (crux) and the top. (It is possible to avoid the last moves of the climb.)

19.   Push-Mi Pull-Yu (F6) is a classic route with uncommonly excellent protection. Start on broken rock (climbed in several different ways) leading up to a prominent crack, beginning twenty feet up with a large pine tree directly above. Climb crack directly (ulti-mately traversing to the large pine tree on the right), scrambling leads up to the top.

20.   Agnostic (F6). To climb this irreverent line, start in a large alcove-chimney, to the left of Push-Mi Pull-Yu. From the alcove-chimney, exit up and left to a ledge, step right and up a steep face to another ledge, then up thin crack and over bulge to the top.

RAINY WEDNESDAY TOWER

The next four sections are actually part of the East Bluffs, but because of their geological peculiarities, I have treated them as smaller but separate climbing areas.

1.   Eave of Destruction (F9) could be your destruc-tion in the event of a fall. Protection is good because of a fixed piton at crux, though it would be a good idea to check it. Start the same as Double Overhang until you are under large ceiling then step right and up.

2.   Double Overhang (F5) is a classic, well-protected route with the final overhang sufficicently exposed to maintain one's interest. Start in prominent crack just left of the block at the base of Resurrection. Climb crack, exit left and up broken rock to a large alcove underneath a prominent overhang (just below the top of the tower). It is often necessary to stop right around a rib to reach this alcove from the broken rock. Climb

RAINY WEDNESDAY TOWER

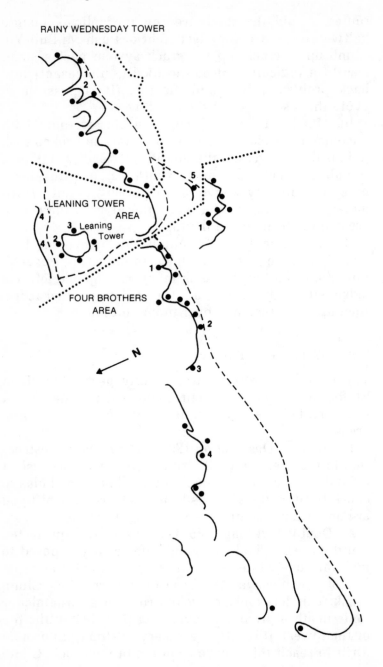

overhang on the left and continue to top of tower. The alcove can also be reached by climbing the face (across the gully from the Green Bulge), fifteen feet left of the regular start.

THE LEANING TOWER

Between Urve's Folly and Wild Horses is a large (broken rock and scree) gully. This is the Leaning Tower Access Gully. The Leaning Tower is located at the top of this gully, along the rail at the top of the bluffs.

1. South Face (F4). Either start from the center or the right corner of face. Climb to the top. The variation starting from the center of the face has been ascended without the use of the hands!

2. North Face (F10). Start from center of the smooth overhanging face. Climb up to a small pocket, then up and left to another pocket, on to the top.

3. East Face or Octagenarian (F7). Start from right edge of face, then up overhanging wall to the top. Ante-Deluvian is a little bit harder. Start from left edge of face, then up to the top.

4. The Tombstone across the trail and north from the Leaning Tower is one of the local bouldering areas. Many variations on its short face are possible. A traverse of the wall provides an interesting route.

5. The Friction Slab below Orgasm should not be missed for its many short routes and boulder problems (good area for the novice). Both the right and left sides of the Slab have been ascended "no-hands."

THE FOUR BROTHERS

The Four Brothers are found by fully descending the Leaning Tower Access Gully and continuing down to the bottom of the lower outcrop. Except for Zot!, an F7

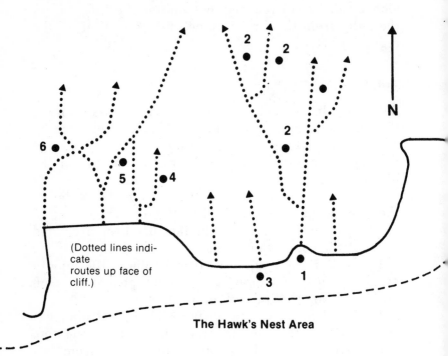

(Dotted lines indicate routes up face of cliff.)

The Hawk's Nest Area

climb, the area is a good one for beginning leaders, offering a multitude of nut placements.

1. The Pretzel (F6). Start in first prominent corner left of the Leaning Tower Access Gully. The corner overhangs for the first fifteen feet. Climb up one corner to a resting stance, then follow crack above to the top.

2. Beginner's Delight (F5) is an aptly named climb with decent exposure. Avoid placing too many pitons as the inevitable rope drag will considerably raise the standard. This is a classic route. Start in cracks left of Beginner's Demise. Many variations are possible at the start. Climb up angling right to corner, traverse right (where most feasible) around corner, then directly to the top.

3. Hero's Fright (F7). Start on the extreme left side of the Beginner's Delight buttress, at the broken rock. (It is possible to start Beginner's Delight here, then a traverse to the right.) There is a prominent crack above near the left corner of face. Climb up to crack, then follow crack closely to the top.

4. Bloody Mary (F9). The gigantic ceiling on this route was originally surmounted with the use of two aid pitons. These were destined to be eliminated. The loose band of rock adds to the fun by causing intense discomfiture—to the mind. Start in an "alcove" just left of Death and Disfiguration. If you cannot find the base of this climb, look around for the ceiling. It is an obvious overhanging bulge of loose rock with a meaty crack running up through the center. Climb up until directly below crack in ceiling, follow the crack (hand jamming and face holds) closely over the ceiling to an awkward stance, continue up and left to a prominent ledge. (The broad ledge of Death and Transfiguration and Death and Disfiguration can be reached by stepping right.) The steep wall above is climbed directly.

THE HAWK'S NEST

This area was probably so named because of the presence of hawks soaring in the thermals that rise from the Devil's Lake basin. The left side of the Hawk's Nest and the start of Scylla, Charybdis, and Coronary are identified by a huge block forming an inside corner facing right toward the main wall. The main wall itself is steep and apparently smooth, thus affording some of the more continuous climbing at Devil's Lake.

1. The Funnel (F6) provides access to three routes above. Start at the prominent groove or cleft with a crack behind a tree. The entire cliff is only about twenty-feet high. Small bushes are visible above. Climb up cleft to broken rock.

2. The Funnel/The Ramp (F6) is another classic. The

only difficult move is wellprotected so you need not worry. Start at the top of the Funnel. Step left and up a short groove, pass a short step (crux) to the prominent slab above, then up a short inside corner on the right to a ledge. Escape left or follow either Exit or Walpurgisnacht to top.

3. Vivesection (F10). Start beneath an overhang five feet above the ground. This overhang caps a small inside corner facing right, fifteen feet left of the Funnel. Conquer the overhang, then at (A) climb straight up cracks to top. Or, follow Exit to the top. A variation: at (A) above overhang, exit left to the upper seciton of Alpha Centauri.

4. Anomie (F8). Climb up ten feet right of Charybdis into an alcove fifteen feet above the ground. Climb out of the alcove up to the right, proceeding to the top on small ledges.

5. Charybdis (F7) is a magnificent line. The climbing is very continuous but well protected. Start at the base of steep wall fifteen feet right of prominent inside corner. Ascend to a small ledge ten feet up, then up slightly higher to a stance. From here a long crack angles up to the right. Follow this crack directly to the top.

6. Coronary (F7) presents an unhappy, unfortunate problem. If the loose block (a crucial hand and foot hold) pulls out, so will your protection. See if you can circumvent this one. Start in prominent inside corner facing right (see Charybdis) and go up corner to a broad ledge. (This ledge can be reached by scrambling around the huge block.) Exit up and right (an interesting mantle) to a comfortable ledge. (This ledge is the same as on Scylla.)

Devil's Doorway

The Devil's Doorway Massif is the largest and most

expansive cliff area at Devil's Lake. When seen from the camp ground at the south end of the lake, its two hundred-foot height is very impressive. Despite first appearance, the area is quite broken up. The tallest vertical walls are about sixty feet. The unique feature of the area is the possibility of multipitch rock climbs, mountain-type scrambling, and problems in route finding.

The Massif is divided by a very large gully into two areas: the Major Mass and the Minor Mass. The Major Mass is larger both vertically and horizontally and contains the distinctive Devil's Doorway rock formation. Most of the rock climbs are in this area.

The Major Mass is divided into the Upper and Lower bands. In between is a large ledge system, which in some places contains a twenty-foot middle band of rock. The buttresses of both bands of the Major Mass are numbered from east to west. Some of the buttresses are also given names. The Minor Mass is to the northeast of the Major Mass.

The Upper Band and the Doorway are best approached by hiking up the Middle East Bluffs trail, now called Devil's Doorway Trail. From the top of the trail, go left (west) to the Devil's Doorway Scenic View Trail and take this trail down the rock stairs to the left. This trail goes along the top of the Third, Fourth, and Fifth buttresses and along the base of Devil's Doorway.

The Lower Band is approached from below by hiking up the talus and by taking the Devil's Doorway Trail up part way, then cutting across the talus and scree until reaching the Keyhole Buttress (look for the very large pine tree). From the top of the Upper Band, slide down the very large gully separating the Major and Minor masses and circle around to the right to the base of the Lower Band.

The Minor Mass is reached from below by hiking up

the trail, then cutting across the talus to the base of the area. From above, descend the large gully between the Major Mass and Minor Mass.

The climbs listed for this area are only suggested. Many variations and other routes are known. The ratings are tentative. The true ratings will have to be established by consensus.

Major Mass of Devil's Doorway

Devil's Doorway has many interesting climbs. It is well worth a half day of fun and frolic. Constructed in 1929 by the Civilian conservation Corps (CCC), it is the scene of many dramatic demonstrations of rock climbing techniques to the passing tourists. A large eye bolt on top is useful as a belay and rappel anchor. Traditionally, the Northwest Ledges or the Doorway Chimney is used to ascend to set up belays. The routes are listed from right to left around the formation. There are a number of climbs around the Devil's Doorway. One of the best is Impossible Crack (F7). Getting into the hanging jam crack is half the battle. Start inside the doorway on a good ledge, work up the wall to the right of the crack, then swing into the crack, and climb to top. An F8 variation begins from the bottom, passing the overhang without using the good ledge on the right.

Upper Band

The Three Kings are three large blocks forming a ridge at the easternmost end of the Upper Band. They can be found by going west on the main trail along the top of the bluffs, then taking the Devil's Doorway side trail down some steps (you are now considerably east of the Doorway itself). At this point the Kings will be south of you. By descending the gully to the left of the

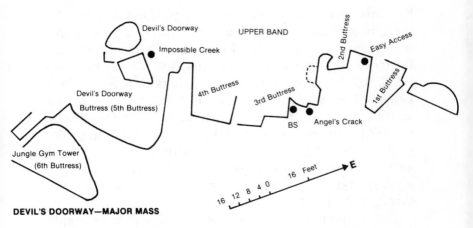

DEVIL'S DOORWAY—MAJOR MASS

trail a short distance and traversing west, the base of the Kings and the First and Second buttresses can be reached.

A better route down is Easy Access on the First Buttress. This buttress has a small boulder sitting on the top, forming an overhang on the west face. Second Buttress is nearly behind the third. Third Buttress is the prominent outcropping directly in front of the notch that the Devil's Doorway side trail passes, just east of the Doorway itself. Angels Crack and BS, located on this buttress, are among the traditional favorite climbs in the Doorway area.

The Angels Crack (F6) route ascends the dihedral on the south side of the buttress. It is marked by an arrowhead slab (crux) two-thirds of the way up the inside corner. Exit to the right of the small "ship's prow," just above the arrowhead slab.

The Fourth Buttress is the rounded buttress between the Third and Devil's Doorway. Devil's Doorway Buttress (Fifth Buttress) is the outcropping on which the Devil's Doorway formation stands.

Lower Band

Keyhole Buttress, being the eastern-most buttress of the Lower Band, will be the First Buttress (for counting purposes). It is also known as the Needle's Eye Buttress. A typical through-the-Keyhole route is to climb the Sunken Slab (F5) to a belay on Scree-Tree Ledge, then ascend through the Keyhole (F5) to the south face of the Keyhole Buttress and the face to the top (F4). Another is to climb Easy Street Chimney (F4) to Picnic Point Ledge, or to a slightly higher ledge, and belay. Traverse at the pine tree on the east face (F4) to a belay stance on Scree-Tree Ledge. From here, ascend through the Keyhole as in the first climb.

The Sunken Slab route starts well up in an inside corner, the most northerly on the Buttress. From the start, you can look through the Keyhole. A belay is often superfluous here as protection is unneeded. Begin on the twenty-five-foot slab on the right and angle up

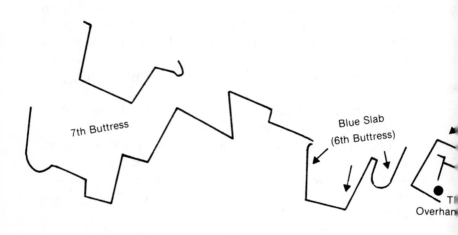

7th Buttress

Blue Slab
(6th Buttress)

T
Overhan

DEVIL'S DOORWAY—MAJOR MASS

to the left. Exit left to Scree-Tree Ledge. Belay from the small birch tree. Extreme care is necessary on this ledge to avoid dislodging the loose rock on climbers or belayers below.

A great climb route on the Red Slab (Fourth) Buttress is TM Overhang (F8). Getting up to the overhang is the tough part. Climb the prominent crack on the east face to a resting place just below the overhang. Reach out for the good holds above the overhang, then merely pull yourself up until footholds are found. It is possible to exit to the left of the overhang.

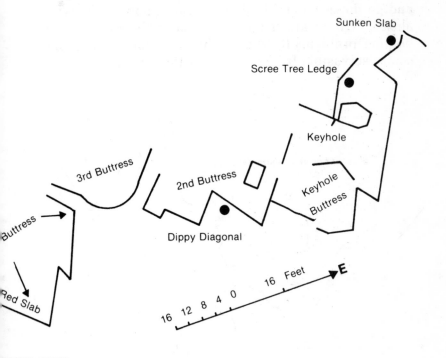

OWER BAND

Minor Mass of Devil's Doorway

The prime route in this area is B-Minor Mass. The imaginative climber will readily discover others.

B-Minor Mass (F5) is a delightful two-pitch climb to the top of a small pinnacle. Begin on the face to the right of the lowest point of the Minor Mass. Ascend the fifteen-foot wall, then traverse left on a good ledge to a small overhang. Belay over the overhang (or rope friction will become unbearable). From the belay, traverse right and climb the inside corner then scramble to the top of the pinnacle. Descend to the Saddle (F3) and go down on either side of it, or climb on the wall ahead. There are some fine scramble routes and boulder problems farther up the large gully. These are easily accessible from the trail at the top.

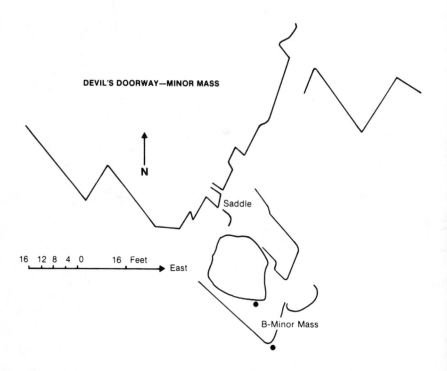

DEVIL'S DOORWAY—MINOR MASS

N

Saddle

16 12 8 4 0   16 Feet
East

B-Minor Mass

Ramsey's Pinnacle, about one hundred yards west of Devil's Doorway is another good climbing area. Two routes start together on the left side of the south face; one goes straight up a jam crack (F6), the other angles right to the chimney. The chockstone at the top is best passed using a layback (F5). Just below Ramsey's is a wall with a variety of climbs. An F7 route goes up the inside corner on the east end of the wall. West of Ramsey's Pinnacle is a ridge offering some F3 climbing and route-finding problems.

The Gorge is a small climbing area reached through the Devil's Doorway Trail (Middle Trail). The pinnacle on the south side of the trail can be ascended from the west (F4). The inside corner on the southeast side is F6. Also try climbing the southeast ridge or chimneying up the Gorge itself. There are several routes on the north face. The far-west face is a traditional climb for beginners.

Balance Rock Area

The following climbs are accessible from the Balance Rock Trail, which zig zags up the boulder field below Balance Rock. For simplicity, assume the boulder field faces directly south. Two-thirds of the way up the boulder field is a good-sized boulder with F5-type routes on its south and east sides. At the op of the boulder field and roughly halfway up the bluff, the trail abuts against a sixty-foot high wall (Balance Rock Wall), then turns west and parallels the base of the wall. Eventually, the rail switches back and climbs to the top of the wall. A short side trail leads to Balance Rock, which is perched at the top of the wall, about fifteen feet west of a point directly above where the trail turns west.

Many of the routes in this area and in the Railroad Tracks Area will be located by referring to various trees (see map). For this reason, it is best to be able to distinguish between five distinct kinds of trees at Devil's Lake: pine, an evergreen; juniper; a small scraggly pine tree; oak, with serrate leaves; birch, with white bark; and "tree," a tree that might not be a pine, juniper, oak, or birch.

Balance Rock Wall

1. Morning After (F10). Climb up starting at the left edge of the forest.

2. Water Marks (F8) is the classic of the area, a fine introduction to face climbing. Start at the head of the trail, go up ten feet, then right six feet to the small triangular pockets. Then head straight up over the bulge to the top. A variation is Watermarks Direct (F9).—Start directly below the triangular pockets.

3. Sunken Pillar or Double Crack (F5). Start in the twin cracks six feet left of the start of Der Glotz and four feet right of the large oak. Follow the obvious line to the top.

The Box Canyon is an eight by ten foot level spot, surrounded by walls of various heights. To get to it, go

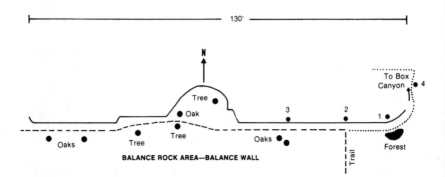

BALANCE ROCK AREA—BALANCE WALL

through the forest, around the cut end of the Balance Rock Wall, and up the slope twenty-five feet. Then turn west and follow a fallen tree up to the floor of the canyon. Or, drop down from Balance Rock to a ledge nine feet below the top of the Balance Rock Wall, then walk east five feet, turn north, and step down five feet into the canyon.

There is a long F3 or F4 route starting at the large broken pine at the east edge of Box Canyon. (Actually it is F5 for the first ten feet.) Climb the cracks for seventeen feet, step right five feet to a chimney, then climb up any way you can.

4. The Balance Climb (F7) goes straight up the lower part of north wall of the canyon, five feet right of the northwest corner. When you reach a small ledge twenty feet up, either traverse left to Balance Rock (F5) or climb straight over the bulge (F7), avoiding the inside corner on the left, or climb the inside corner (F5) passing the Phallic Symbol. The crack on the west wall of Box Canyon is about F6. The face left of it is F8. There's a nice long climb on a northeast facing outside corner, starting twenty feet east of and below the Box Canyon.

Balance Rock Ridge is a series of short pitches, with many variations, leading from Balance Rock to the top of the bluff, two hundred feet above.

RAILROAD TRACKS AREA

Above the eastern shore of the lake, roughly a third of the way from the south shore to the north shore, are a number of outcrops affording excellent climbing. Many are of low elevation, a feature appreciated on hot summer days. Carry a swimming suit in your pack.

The major outcrops are all near the "electric fence," a net that parallels the railroad tracks for a few hundred feet and warns trains of rockslides. A telephone line

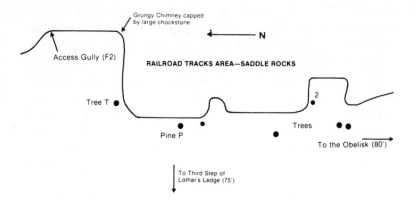

also parallels the tracks, and its poles will be used to locate the climbs in this area. The telephone pole nearest the center of the electric fence is the "equator." The poles south of it are denoted by 1S, 2S, etc., and those north of it by 1N, 2N, etc. Thus, pole 1S is the pole near the south end of the electric fence. The notation 2.7S, 200'), for example, denotes a feature about two hundred feet above the railroad and about seven-tenths of the way from pole 2S to pole 3S.

For simplicity, assume the tracks run exactly north and south. In spite of this simplification, directions are probably correct only to the nearest 45°. Adhere to the tree code established in the previous (Balance Rock) section.

There are three major outcrops: the Saddle Rocks (2.7S to 1.8S, 200'), Birthday Rocks (1.7S to Equator, 100'-50'), and the Amphitheater (2.0N to 2.3N, 20'). Other prominent features are: the Obelisk (2.7S, 200'), a forty-foot spire, ten feet wide at the base; Lothar's Ledges (2.0S, 100' to 200'), a series of three rock steps leading up to the Saddle Rocks; Pseudo Turkshead (1.5S, 200'), a sixty-foot tower capped by a bulging block, visible from (1.9S, 100'); the Great Dihedral (0.9S, 100'), a sixty-five-foot "W" facing the inside corner; and Index Rock (2.0S, 0'), a boulder with a well-defined ridge pointing up to the right wall of the Amphitheater.

Many of the climbs in this area are scarcely used, so expect inaccuracies and inconsistencies in ratings. The more difficult ones are usually rated F8, F9, or F10, with no embellishments, exceptions being the more popular routes.

Lothar's Ledges, named for Lothar Kolbig, who climbed in the 1940s and 1950s, is a series of three rock steps, starting at (2.0S, 100'). It is a good place for beginners, since each step has at least one easy route.

First Step: For the SW Face (F3) any route will do. For West Face (F8) go up the face just right of the northwest corner. A variation (for short people) is up the southwest corner for about six feet and traverse left to join the west face route. East Face (F4) is up the right side of the face past the pine. From the top of the First Step, you can step down the southeast corner to the notch.

Second Step: Short Man's Anguish (F7) is reached by leaning across to the Second Step from the top of the First Step. (This much is possible if you're 5'5" or taller.) If shorter than 5'10", bellyflop into the Second Step, crash backwards to the First Step or call for help, depending on whether your belay is from above, behind, or nonexistent. If 5'10" or taller grab the bucket, swing across, and climb up. NW Corner (F3) actually has two distinct routes, both of them easy. For West Face (F8), go up the center of the face, joining Short Man's Anguish halfway up.

Third Step: For SW Corner (F5), climb the crack on the "W" face, step right, then up to the top. A variation (F6)—at the top of the crack, go straight over the bulge. From the top of the Third Step, follow a rib of rock east seventy-five feet to the large pine (P) at the base of the Saddle Rocks.

Saddle Rocks provides some of the most enjoyable climbing at the lake.

1.   Rogers Roof (F8). Climb the corner and wall four feet to the right of the pine (P) to a small platform below the crack in the roof. Jam over the roof (F9 or so if you don't use a knee). Continue up past a confusing bulge to the top. A bong is advised at the roof, since the crack rejects nuts.

2.   Debauchery (F8) is the third best climb at Devil's Lake. It has never been led, thanks to the unprotected F7 move thirty feet up. Climb on or near the corner for twenty-five feet, then step a few feet left and pull up to a comfortable ledge. Above this point the corner is ill-defined. Continue up and slightly right, over the crux and up into a shallow concavity for the final ten feet. A direct route, avoiding the concavity, may be possible. A variation (F8) has the same start, but stay on the steep face right of the corner until the ledge thirty feet up. This is slightly harder, but may afford a little protection. The Obelisk is a tower about eighty feet south of Ptolemy. Its top is separated from the main wall by a jumpable gap. (Use a belay the first time you try it.) There is a quarter-inch bolt on the top for top roping. The climb has not been led to date, mainly because of the relative scarcity of daring climbers in this section. Start at the southwest corner, proceed diagonally across the west face, and then up the northwest corner to the top. The climb is F7, except for the first move, which is F9. A strenuous alternate start on the northwest corner may now be easier than the standard start.

The north face of the Obelisk has been climbed by stepping to it from the main wall. The rating is F10 to F5, depending on how high up you step over. The southeast corner has also been done.

The buttress just north of the Obelisk also has three good climbs.

BIRTHDAY ROCKS

Birthday Crack (F7) was an F6 climb until a chockstone was pulled out in the 1960s. Start in the crack eight feet left of the Great Dihedral. Climb the crack system to the top.

There are a number of climbs on the wall left of the Birthday Crack. For example, one can climb the upper half of the wall just left of the crack. There are a couple of decent F6 or F7 cracks thirty to forty feet left of the Great Dihedral.

Caesarian Tower (F9) forms the right wall of the Great Dihedral. From Pederasty Ledge, climb the sharp west corner of the tower to a wide ledge halfway up. Swing precariously up and to the right to the overhanging upper half of the corner, then shinny to the top of the tower. Now rappel off, chopping the bolts on the northwest face as you descend. The first half is easier if you climb the inside corner to the right of the usual start.

THE AMPHITHEATER

Everyone whose climbing experience has been limited to Devil's Lake should spend a day climbing in this section before venturing out into the rest of the world. The climbs here are in some indescribable way very different from the "typical" Devil's Lake climb.

The Amphitheater consists of two walls forming a wide angle and separated by a gully. There is a pillar (appropriately called the Pillar) reaching about halfway up the left wall, just left of the gully. Easy access to the top of the Amphitheater can be made by the slopes somewhat to the north and south of the whole outcrop.

West Bluffs Area

Climbs on the West Bluffs are typical of Devil's Lake, with perhaps a little more broken rock, yielding a higher proportion of moderate routes. Remember on northern exposures that holds are apt to be down sloping because of the prevailing tilt of the rocks. Rocks for climbing on the West Bluffs are widely scattered, often consisting of small outcroppings separated by wooded slopes. The extensive greenery can make them difficult to spot. A few sections of the West Bluffs, however, have a good concentration of climbs.

If you arrive at the lake from the west on the South Shore Road, you travel down some switch backs. At the point when you get to the lake level, there is a short road that branches off to the left (east), then turns north. Its length is about five hundred yards. At the end of the road are about four cottages, right on the lake. Use these as a reference guide. At the end of the road is the beginning of the trail called the Tumbled Rocks Trail, which goes along the west shore of Devil's Lake. It connects the north shore with the south shore. Use this as the access to the West Bluffs area or park just off the park (main) road and hike up the West Bluff Trail.

Misery Group

The Misery Group of rocks is in the region above the cottages at the southwest corner of Devil's Lake. The group includes Porkchop Buttress, about two hundred feet above the northern-most cottage. This has two relatively long routes, each about seventy-feet long (F5 and F6). At the local summit of the region is Fat Man's Misery, a forty-foot rock that leans against the summit wall. The traditional route starts on the wall behind the south end of the rock and continues in the narrow chimney above the south end. There are many other climbs around this section and nearby rocks.

The West Bluff at Devil's Lake as seen from the Tumbled Rocks Trail. *(Alan Bagg)*

TURK'S HEAD GROUP

The Turk's Head group is the prominent section high up on the south half of the bluff. For a convenient approach, start from the southwest corner of Devil's Lake and follow the West Bluff or Summit trail to where it breaks out of the woods and overlooks the lake. From this point, Cleopatra's Needle is visible about fifty feet below the rim of the summit walls. The southwest side of this pinnacle is a popular F5 climb. A permanent ring at the top can be used for rappelling off. The walls of the amphitheater that surround Cleopatra's Needle are densely covered with routes. Reasoner's Wall and Turk's Head, a jutting tower, form a northerly extension of the Amphitheater. (Reasoner's Wall has an obvious crack, two pitches separated by a ledge.) A recommended variation on the upper pitch is a smooth face just north of the crack (F7).

PROSPECT POINT RAMPART

The rampart is the summit cliff on the central section on the West Bluff. Prospect Point is on the Summit Trail, roughly midway between the north and south shores. It affords a splendid vista of the entire lake. The rampart extends north from this point, averaging about eighty feet in height, but for the most part, climbs are interrupted by benches and wide ledges. Three hundred feet north of Prospect Point is a geodetic survey marker along the Summit Trail. Several long continuous routes can be located from this marker. Fifty feet to the south is Great Chimney, a F4 access route, formed by a narrow promontory slanting off to the north. The east side of the promontory has long chimney and crack routes, in the F6 to F7 range. One hundred feet north of the marker is Lost Face, about a hundred feet high. The standard route follows cracks and F6 ledges.

Roger Wiegand claims that Lost Face is the best climb on the entire West Bluff. He says it is a classic, even better than the extremely popular Brinton's Crack on the East Bluffs. Offering a variety of climbing technique opportunities, Lost Face is located close to Prospect Point.

PROSPECT POINT TOWERS

Prospect Point Towers forms a ridge that extends up the middle third of the bluff below Prospect Point. When ascended from the bottom, it provides a multiple-pitch route for several fine towers and walls. These climbs are recommended for the East Bluffs areas, proceeding the way the climber would encounter them going from he east to the west.

THE WALL

Monster
The Thing

MAIN SUMMIT WALL

Last Gasp (F8)
Easy Overhang (F5)
Zig Zag (F6)
Sometime Crack (F9)
The Stretcher (F9)
Upper Diagonal (F9)
The Pedastal (F5)
Condolences (F7)
Congratulations Crack (F9)
The Spine (F5)
Gill's Crack (F9)
Boy Scout (F4)
Brinton's Crack (F6)

Brinton's Direct(F8)
Berkeley (F6)
Thoroughfare (F10)
Vascillation (F7)
Full Stop (F6)
Schizophrenia (F6)
Moderation (F4)
Anemia (F4)
Peter's Project (F7)
Michael's Project (F7)
The Black Rib (F10)
Lichen (F4)
Tibia Crack (F8)
Horticulture (F5)
The Cheatah (F9)
Push-Mi Pull-Yu (F6)
Agnostic (F7)
Coatimundi Crack (F6)

RAINY WEDNESDAY TOWER

False Alarm Jam (F1)
Double Overhang (F5)

FOUR BROTHERS

The Pretzel (F6)
Beginner's Delight (F5)
Hero's Fright (F7)
Bloody Mary (F9)

HAWK'S NEST AREA

Happy Hunting Ground (F10)
The Funnel/Bucket Brigade (F6)
The Funnel/ The Ramp (formerly the Slab) (F6)
Vivisection (F10)
Anomie (F8)

Charybdis (F7)
Coronary (F7)

Devils Doorway—Major Mass

Angel's Crack (F6)
Mary Jane (F8)
Easy Street/Keyhole (F5)
King's Corner (F6)
Dippy Diagonal (F6)
Red Slab (F5)
TM Overhang (F8)
7th Buttress/Jungle Gym (F5)
Playground (F7)

Devils Doorway—Minor Mass

Pigeon Roof (F6)
B-Minor Mass (F5)
Green Ledges (F7)

Balanced Rocks Area

Water Marks (F8)
Der Glotz (F9)
Sunken Pillar (F5)

Railroad Tracks Area

Snedegar's Nose (F7)
Cop Out (F10)
Pine Tree Step Across (F6)
Horner's Corner (F5)
Birthday Crack (F7)
Caeserian Tower (F8)
Rogers Roof (F8)
Treachery (F7)
Primax Surprise (F?—that's the surprise)

ACCOMMODATIONS and OTHER ATTRACTIONS

There are many adequate accommodations in the Devil's Lake area, primarily campgrounds and motels, but they are in tremendous demand throughout the summer and it's simply impossible to find a campsite or room without a reservation during July and August.

There are three separate campgrounds located on the north and south shores of Devil's Lake. Together they provide a total of 458 individual sites. In addition, there is an organized-group, tent camping site and an indoor group camp on the south shore.

The state-run public campgrounds located in the park are the first to fill, since people from all over the country flock to the famous park. A number of private campgrounds serve as a backup for the large crowds, but are also nearly always full during the peak summer months. Don't plan on coming to the park without a reservation in summer.

Reserving a state park campsite is accomplished by filling out a form available from any state park or forest, the Wisconsin Tourist Information Bureau in Chicago, or by writing directly to the DNR, box 450, Madison, Wisconsin 53707. Reservations are not accepted on the south shore; they can be made for the north shore sites from May 15 through Labor Day. Reservations are required for the indoor group camp and outdoor group campground. Campers using individual sites must register at the park office in advance. The office will assign sites.

Groceries and light snacks are available at the park concession stands. Other supplies can be obtained in Baraboo, three miles north of the park. Ice machines are located on both the north and south shores. There are no laundry facilities located in the park but laundromats are available in Baraboo.

Showers are located in the bathhouses and toilet buildings on both the north and south shores. There are three major designated picnic grounds in the park with associated picnic shelters. Water, tables, grills, and fireplaces are available.

Private campgrounds located in the area are:

Baraboo: Fox Hills Campground—100 sites, showers
 Skillet Creek Farm—175 sites, showers
 Merry Mac's Camp 'N—141 sites, showers
 Shady Trail Campground—30 sites
 Terrytown Campground—50 sites, showers
 Tuck-A-Way Farm Campground—120 sites,
 showers
Lone Rock: Flying J Campground—40 sites, showers
 Madison: Goodland Park (CH "M")—25 sites
 KOA—113 sites, showers
 Token Creek County Park (SH 51)—30 sites,
 showers
Reedsburg: Lighthouse Rock Campground—70 sites,
 showers
Sauk City: Blackhawk Ridge Wilderness Camp—50
 sites, showers
 Snuffy's Campsite—145 sites, showers
Spring Green: Bob's Riverside Camp—70 sites,
 showers

(Also see Gibraltar Rock and Abelman's Gorge "Accommodations and other attractions" listings.)

Gibraltar Rock

DESCRIPTION

Gibraltar Rock is a rather popular sandstone cliff, somewhat less than one hundred fifty feet high, located in the Columbia County park of the same name. There is a paved but very tightly curved road to the top of the cliff, with a parking lot for about a half-

The larger outcrops at Gibraltar Rock overlook the Wisconsin River and offer excellent climbing and rappelling opportunities. *(Alan Bagg)*

dozen vehicles. This wooded park, open year round, makes an excellent place to picnic and spend the day climbing. The road is not always plowed in winter, which necessitates a hike into the climb site. The top of the cliff affords an excellent view of the most picturesque farm country in the state. From one point, Lake Wisconsin, an enlargement of the Wisconsin River, can be seen to the northwest. A few copies of an eight-page pamphlet written by Roger Wiegand in 1971 are still in the hands of Wisconsin Climbers of that era. The mimeographed work, called "Climber's and Fisherman's Guide to Gibraltar Rock," humorously describes twenty-one climbs Wiegand and his friends have made on the cliffs. The Wisconsin Hoofers (see climbing clubs in Chapter 4) may be able to direct you to a copy, even though the pamphlets are not currently in print.

There are a number of good crack-climbing routes on the upper sections of rock, though the lower portions tend to be somewhat rotten. A selection of nuts can give good protection for most climbs. There are a couple of half-day routes and some aid climbing at Gibraltar Rock to challenge more advanced climbers.

LOCATION

Gibraltar Rock County Park is located about four miles west of the town of Lodi. Road signs in and around Lodi will direct you to the park if approaching it from the south or east. From the north or west, take either SH 188 or 113 to CH "V" and follow V either east (from 188) or west (from 113) to the park road

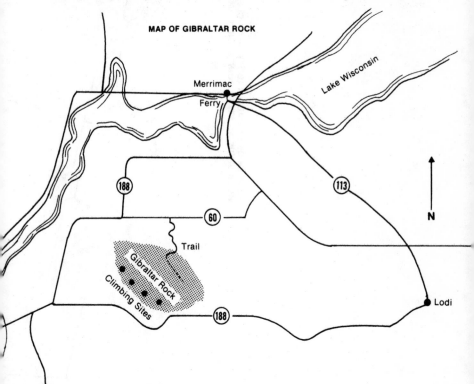

MAP OF GIBRALTAR ROCK

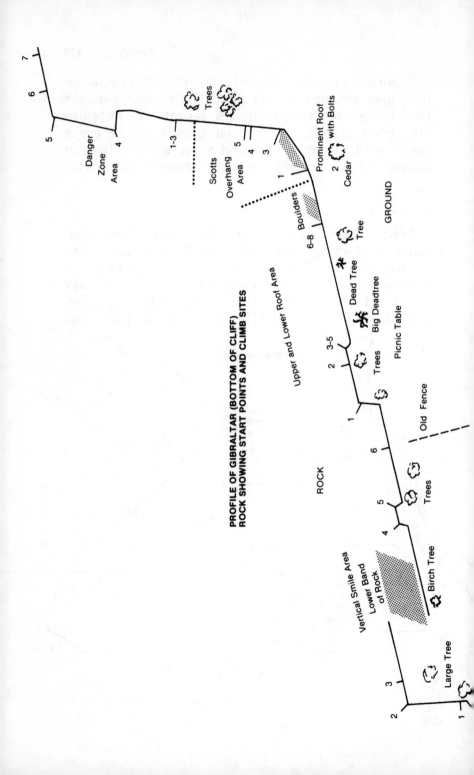

PROFILE OF GIBRALTAR (BOTTOM OF CLIFF)
ROCK SHOWING START POINTS AND CLIMB SITES

(labeled CH "VA" on official county maps). State highway maps do not show Gibraltar Rock, but it is on the 15' USGS Baraboo quad. Follow the park road all the way to the top and park on the loop provided. A short trail leads from the parking lot to the cliff.

CLIMBING

There are four climbing areas at Gibraltar Rock Park, all of which must be descended to, using a variety of routes. Most will take a bit of searching. One of the easiest ways to reach the bottom of the cliff is to walk around to the northeast side of the park from either end and down the much easier back slope (the whole cliff section of Gibraltar Rock is less than a quarter-mile wide). You can also negotiate to the bottom by following the trail from the parking area until one part branches down along the edge of the cliff. There are several spots here where a short rappel or scramble will get you down to where the climbs begin.

The upper half of Gibraltar Rock is solid, making for good climbing, although knobs and small holds are weathered and sometimes break off. A majority of the routes follow cracks, and nuts usually provide excellent protection. A selection of chocks, including a no. 6 or no. 7 hex and a few cabled nuts, is about all you need for most of the routes.

The climbing areas described in Wiegand's booklet all begin at the left of the wide, tree-filled area that divides the cliff (from below, looking toward the rock). In this area the hillside comes up farther, so the cliff itself is only forty to sixty feet high.

SCOTTS OVERHANG AREA

A prominent roof to the left of the tree-filled spot is Scotts Overhang, thirty to forty feet above the ground.

It juts out about fifteen feet and serves as a landmark (marked by an incomplete bolt ladder). To the right of Scotts Overhang, the ground slopes upward, making the climbs correspondingly shorter.

Five of the most difficult climbs are found here, some of them half-day affairs (Grade II) with difficult aid pitches tossed in. Cedar Jest, Bishops Sister, Bishopric, and Sonofabishop offer a variety of climbing technique challenges. Cedar Jest has been extolled as the "most aesthetic line" at Gibraltar.

UPPER and LOWER ROOF AREA

About sixty feet left of Scotts Overhang and about fifty feet above the ground, two rectangular roofs, called the Upper Roof and Lower Roof, jut out about three feet. They are both about eight feet long, but the Upper Roof (on the right) is slightly larger.

Interesting twin to either side of a big ledge ascend two dihedrals in the recessed wall, about one hundred feet left of Scotts Overhang. The routes are named Locomotive and Mother Bear. Six other routes can be found here by consulting the map.

VERTICAL SMILE AREA

One hundred fifty feet left of Scotts Overhang is a narrow, rotten looking chimney called the Vertical Smile. An old fence sets within a couple of feet from the cliff's edge and left of this the ground starts sloping up again. About twenty-five feet left of Vertical Smile, in another recessed (and smaller) section, are a few more good climbs, but the rock is quite broken and overgrown.

About a hundred feet left of Vertical Smile is a challenging roof. The crack running through it, Dave's Dive, is near the extreme left end of the cliff on a section of rock almost perpendicular to the main wall.

It's best to study the routes from the top before climbing at Gibraltar Rock. *(Alan Bagg)*

DANGER ZONE AREA

There are a few more climbs to the right and at the head of the tree-filled area, located to the right of Scotts Overhang. The climbs here are somewhat hazardous because tourists who visit the park throw rocks down the cliff. The bottom half of the cliff is fairly rotten, except for the section by Locomotive.

ACCOMMODATIONS AND OTHER ATTRACTIONS

Rooms and campsites in the Gibraltar Rock area are basically the same ones that are found in the Devil's Lake area, with the addition of three campgrounds near Lodi:

Gannon's Birchwood Resort and Campground—373
    sites, showers.
Gaukel's Resort Beausite—215 sites, showers.
Smokey Hollow Campground—110 sites, showers.

(See Devil's Lake "Accommodations and other attractions").

Climb routes by name for Gibraltar Rock.

Vertical Smile Area
  Dave's Dive (F8)
  The Slot (F5)
  The Hole (F6)
  Scotfree (F9)
  Vertical Smile (F8)
Upper and Lower Roof Area
  Mother Bear (F7)
  Milhaus (F9)
  Locomotive (F8)
  Face It (F9)
  Winter Solstice (F6, A2)
  Birch Tree (F8)
  Classic (F7)
  Cop Out (F7)

Scotts Overhang Area
  Bearded Clam (F8)
  Cedar Jest II (F7)
  Bishops Sister II (F8, A3)
  Bishopric II (F6, A3)
  Sonofabishop (A3)

Danger Zone Area
  Flying Machine (F8)
  Dead Tree (A2)
  Six Feet Right (F8)
  Garrote (F7)
  Cloaca (F5)
  Chianti (F6, A1)
  Burgundy (F5)

Abelman's Gorge

DESCRIPTION

Abelman's Gorge, a two hundred-foot notch cut by the Baraboo River in Sauk County, displays an exceptional panorama of rock types and geological structures found in southern Wisconsin. It affords the adventurous climber a good change of pace from the overstudied Devil's Lake area.

The whole south-central Wisconsin region was virtually left in tact after the last glacier moved through. This makes the topographic features of the terrain very different from the rest of the state's geology. Scattered oak, red cedar, pine, hemlock, and patches of prairie plants dress the bluffs, and along the river bottoms is a diverse and strikingly beautiful display of spring flowers.

The gorge is easy to overlook in attempting to explore new climbing sites, since it is less than a mile long and is overshadowed by the more popular Devil's Lake. Part of the gorge (6.7 acres) is owned by the University of Wisconsin, deeded to them by the Wisconsin chapter of the Nature Conservancy, a preservationist group who had the foresight to acquire it a number of years ago.

Frequented by hikers, geology students, and botony buffs who appreciate the ecological mixture of small outcrops that overlook the river, the gorge is near enough to Devil's Lake State Park to be accessible as a side trip, but interesting enough to be done as a completely separate trip—concentrating on the untrammelled routes of an old quartzite quarry, a part of the gorge itself. Climbing has not yet become one of the big attractions there, so many days a group of climbers can have the area all to itself.

Sauk County is prime recreation country, offering probably the most varied activities, in addition to rock climbing, in the whole state. Other nearby activities and attractions are listed in the "Accommodations and other attractions" section.

Fortunately for climbers, this area is close to major cities: Milwaukee (118 miles), Green Bay (150 miles), Minneapolis (230 miles), Chicago (240 miles), and Des Moines (300 miles).

LOCATION

Located on the north edge of the town of Rock Springs in Salk County, on SH 136, Abelman's Gorge (also called Rock Springs Narrows on some maps) is fairly easy to find once you know it's there.

There are basically two climb sites described here. They are reached by parking at a turnout along Highway 136. You will recognize the parking area on the east side since there is a spring there, an excellent water supply for thirsty climbers. Bring some jugs to fill for the trip home. From the spring a short walk west northwest (almost due west, actually) will take you to the major climbing area, an abandoned quarry.

Abelman's Gorge can be found on the North Freedom Wisconsin 15' USGS quad.

CLIMBING

One of the most scenic attractions in the Baraboo Valley, Abelman's Gorge stretches north and south above the Baraboo River, about three-quarters of a mile in length. The gorge stands like a sentinel, or the ever faithful watchdog, in whose memory is locked years of stone quarrying. Baraboo quartzite, the predominant rock type, has been mined there right up to the present time. The east side of the gorge is private property, owned by the Chicago and North Western Railway. The large quarry is operated on contract by a firm from Minneapolis. Climbing is off-limits on the east; on the west side, the abandoned quarry, which ceased operations about thirty or forty years ago, is climbable.

ABANDONED QUARRY AREA

This old quarry is geologically the most interesting section of the whole gorge. Sheer two hundred-foot quartzite faces will test the skills of more advanced climbers and those who like the challenge of route finding.

UW PLOT

Just northeast of the railroad tracks and Highway 136

bridge across the river is the property owned by the university. This area makes a fine place for rock scrambling and is also a nice place to picnic if an all-day outing is made of the quarry climbing.

ACCOMMODATIONS AND OTHER ATTRACTIONS

Accommodations are about the same as those offered at Devil's Lake. The park offers the best place to camp, but the same cautions apply as were mentioned in the Devil's Lake section. Motel rooms in the Wisconsin Dells Area to the northeast are slightly higher priced than normal because of the heavy tourist trade and are scarce in the summer (reservations mandatory).

Weidman Park, a scenic wayside for picnicking, is only a mile west of Rock Springs on SH 154. On rainy days or weekends, a number of area attractions are available to pass the time. They are very worthwhile seeing if you have the time.

Tower Hill State Park, on SH 213 in Iowa County. There is a unique shot tower that was used during the French and Indian Wars. Shot was formed by dropping hot lead from the tower into cool water. Tower Hill also has camp sites which are not in quite as much demand as at Devil's Lake.

Taliesin, on SH 23, south of Spring Green (admission). Home of Frank Lloyd Wright, includes his home, barns, and architecture school.

House on the Rock, eight miles south of Spring Green on SH 23 (admission). This unique private home, built on a rock, has no two rooms that are architecturally alike. A large collection of interesting roomsize music boxes is a favorite attraction.

Agency House, on SH 33, one mile northeast of Portage. Here the Surgeon's Quarters and Theatre Historique, on the site of old Fort Winnebago, depict the early history of Wisconsin.

Scenic areas include Parfrey's Gorge, three miles east of SH 113, north of Merrimac, and two miles west of SH 78, north of Merrimac. This is a nature-study area managed by the state of Wisconsin.

Pewitt's Nest, three miles west of Baraboo on CH "W" is another scenic area on Skillet Creek. A picturesque falls is located a short distance upstream on private land.

part 3

4

Group Climbing: Midwest Climbing Clubs

There are a number of benefits one gets from belonging to a climbing group: access to capable instructors (sometimes free), availability of climbing partners, climbing trip opportunities with shared expenses, regularity of workouts on the rocks, and certainly a sense of comraderie that climbers enjoy.

Throughout the Midwest, largely centered on college campuses, fraternities of climbers with outdoorsy sounding names have developed over the years. Some of these have only a handful of members and offer limited services, while others, like the 630-member Iowa Mountaineers, are large, well-organized groups offering a wealth of activities and services to its members.

Even though you are not a college student, you may consider joining a club. Here is a listing of the known climbing clubs in the Midwest.

Chicago Mountaineering Club
926 Judson, Apt. 1 W
Evanston, IL 60202
Attention: Madelon Clymo

This club has two hundred members who schedule rock climbing outings every third week to Devil's Lake State Park in Wisconsin. Memberships are open to the public, but prospective members must attend three club outings as a guest and be approved by club members. The $12 annual membership fee does not include camp fees.

Instruction for beginning rock climbers is handled by rope leaders assigned by the club. Club members also take a trip to mountains in the western United States once every two years.

Hoofers Outing Club
University of Wisconsin
800 Langdon Street
Madison, WI 53706

The Hoofers are a loosely organized mountaineering and outdoor activities group headquartered at the University of Wisconsin in Madison. The club is officially recognized as a university organization.

Memberships are open to nonstudents at the cost of $15 for annual dues. Summer memberships are $8. Beginning instruction in rock climbing is available on club outings through club members. "Rope fees" are collected for this. Club members usually climb year round on weekends at Devil's Lake.

Other club activities also include kayaking, canoeing, backpacking, and bicycling.

Iowa Mountaineers, Inc.
P.O. Box 163
Iowa City, IA 52240

The Mountaineers are the largest organized group in

the Midwest, with members numbering approximately 630. The group is officially part of the University of Iowa, but is open to alumni and associate members who are not students. Annual dues are $5 and the club offers beginner, intermediate, and advanced aid-climbing classes.

The club climbs at Palisades-Kepler and Backbone state parks in Iowa, Mississippi Palisades in Illinois, and Devil's Lake, as well as the Needles in South Dakota and western mountain ranges in the United States and Canada. The group also sponsors major summer climbing camps for instruction. (See Climbing Schools in Chapter 5.)

Iowa State University Mountaineering Club
107 State Gym
Ames, IA 50010

The club at Iowa State has twenty-five members and is also officially connected to the university, but non-student memberships are available. Annual dues are $6. The ISU Mountaineering Club offers beginning and intermediate instruction and climbs at Ledges State Park in Iowa, Mississippi Palisades, and Devil's Lake.

Minnesota Rovers Outing Club
P.O. Box 14133
University Station
Minneapolis, MN 55414

The Rovers have four hundred members and have a subgroup called the University of Minnesota Rovers, an official part of the university, which holds its own meetings and has its own officers. General Rovers, memberships are open to the public for $7 annually. About half the total members are students.

The Rovers offer all levels of instruction, including aid climbing, and the goup climbs at Interstate Park in Minnesota, Devil's Lake, Devil's Tower in Wyoming;

and in Mexico, Alaska, Peru, Europe, Nepal, and Canada.

The club is also involved in a number of other outdoor activities, such as backpacking, canoeing, spelunking, and keeps group trips small so as not to damage the environment. Group trips are lead by capable leaders.

Ohio University Alpine Club
Baker Center
Ohio University
Athens, OH 45701

The forty-member Alpine Club is officially affiliated with Ohio University. Memberships are open to the public at $3 per year. The club offers beginning and intermediate rock climbing classes and climbs at Clifton Gorge in Ohio and Seneca Rocks in West Virginia. Many members climb in other parts of the country and in pit caves in Mexico. The group is involved in other outdoor activities, such as caving, backpacking, canoeing, and cross-country skiing.

Simian Outing Society
Office of Campus Programs and Services
110 Student Services Building
University of Illinois
Champaign, IL 61820

The Simian Outing Society at the Champaign-Urbana campus has thirty student and staff members. Annual dues are $3. The club offers beginning rock climbing classes and climbs on private land in Indiana, at Devil's Lake, Mississippi Palisades, and in the Shawnee National Forest in southern Illinois. The group also takes climbing trips to Colorado and also participates in mountaineering, cross-country skiing, and backpacking.

St. Louis University Grotto
20 North Grand Boulevard
St. Louis, MO 63103
This fifty-member club is an unofficial university student organization whose members climb in Missouri and Illinois. Annual dues are $6. Beginning and intermediate climbing instruction is offered by members. The group also participates in backpacking and cave exploring.

University of Cincinnati Mountaineering Club
Tangeman University Center
Cincinnati, OH 45221
As an official organization of the university, this fifty-member student club charges $7.50 annual dues and offers beginning instruction in rock climbing to members. Club members climb at Clifton Gorge, and Seneca Rocks and Linville Gorge in North Carolina. Other activities of the club include spelunking, canoeing, backpacking, and mountaineering.

5

Going Higher with Climbing Schools

Safe climbing practices to reduce the number of yearly accidents and rescues are essential if climbers are to avoid the restrictions of legislation prohibiting climbing in certain areas or otherwise interfering with the free enjoyment of the sport. It is the responsibility of all climbers to familiarize themselves completely with their equipment and techniques and learn the advantages and limitations of each. It is especially important that climbers avoid placing themselves in situations that are beyond their knowledge, skills, and experience or the limitations of their equipment. Learning from an expert climber is the easiest and safest method of acquiring climbing experience. Novice rock climbers or those who wish to improve faulty techniques would do well to enroll in one of the U.S. climbing schools listed here.

Bob Culp Climbing School
1329 Broadway
Boulder, CO 80302
Director: George Hurley

This school has been in business for seven years and offers two, three, and four half-day climbing classes in rock and ice climbing. Half-day sessions consist of four to six hours of instruction in 2 to 1 or 3 to 1 pupil/instructor ratios. The climbs are taught year round in the Boulder area, primarily at Eldorado Canyon, by a team of seven instructors. Basic and advanced courses are offered, and all equipment is provided. Rock Courses (ratio 3 to 1, cost: more than $50) consist of four half-day lessons for novices. Topics taught include rappelling, belaying, hardware, protection, and boulder climbing. The introductory lesson includes an easy actual climb.

Advanced Rock Course (ratio 2 to 1, cost: more than $50) offers choice of three half-day lessons, two of direct aid or advanced free-face and crack climbing. Third day is spent free climbing.

Ice Climbing is a two-day, very specialized technical ice course spent on frozen waterfalls in Boulder or Clear Creek Canyon. Students must know basic free climbing to enroll. Brochure and details can be requested by mail.

Eastern Mountain Sports Climbing School
Main Street
North Conway, NH 03860
Director: Jim Dunn

The EMS school has been operating since 1968 and offers instruction in all phases of mountaincraft, especially technical rocks and ice climbing, offering beginner, intermediate, and private courses. Clean climbing and flexibility for the student's needs as a climber are emphasized. Classes last about seven hours.

Beginner (ratio: generally 3 to 1, up to 5 to 1, cost:

less then $50) introduces the fundamentals of technical climbing and is intended for people with no technical experience or those who need to brush up on their techniques. The instructor discusses current ideas in climbing: displays various equipment; teaches knots, belaying, and rappelling; and demonstrates free-climbing techniques. Students do a short climb and a rappel, which provide an excellent opportunity to use the ideas and techniques they have practiced throughout the day.

Intermediate (ratio: 3 or 2 to 1, cost: less than $50) is intended for people who have some technical climbing experience and emphasizes complicated, clean, free-climbing techniques. Either one or two multipitched routes (from easy to moderate difficulty) on Cathedral, Whitehorse, or Cannon Cliffs are climbed.

Private (cost; less than $50) for persons interested in specific aspects of climbing, such as direct-aid climbing (using etriers), acquiring leading qualities, or going out alone with an instructor.

Ice Climbing (cost: same as rock climbing) offers beginner and intermediate courses throughout the winter, teaching the latest techniques in icecraft. The French, Austrian, and International (combination of French and Austrian) techniques of using the ice axe and crampons will be taught. The course also covers self arresting, placing ice screws, cutting steps, and the application of these techniques to various climbing conditions.

Exum Guide Service
Box 10
Moose, WY
Director: Glenn Exum
One of the oldest climbing schools in the country (open more than forty-two years), Exum offers a number of specialized one-day courses, from June 11 to September 11 at Jenny Lake in the Grand Teton Na-

tional Park in Wyoming. Courses last about eight hours with a staff of fifteen instructors who teach beginning, intermediate, advanced, and two-day snow and ice mountaineering courses. Student/instructor ratios are kept small.

Basic rock climbing covers knots, rappelling, friction, and other topics. Advanced courses build on and advance this knowledge. Ratio: 10 to 1 beginning, 4 to 1 intermediate, 2 to 1 advanced. Cost: less than $50. Equipment included in price of course.

Fantasy Ridge Alpinism
P. O. Box 2106
Estes Park, CO 80517
Director: Mike Covington

Fantasy Ridge provides a number of specialized one-day courses year round at Rocky Mountain National Park at Estes Park, Colorado. Courses last from six to ten hours, with group instruction and a guided climb. A competent staff of thirteen instructors teach all classes, beginner through advanced. Student/teacher ratios are determined by course difficulty and are kept small. Equipment is included in price of the course.

All rock climbing classes emphasize the use of clean climbing techniques. In addition to rock climbing, snow and ice, mountaineering, and expedition trips and instruction are also available. Rock climbing classes include:

Basic Rock (ratio: 5 to 1, cost: less than $50) for novices with little or no experience. Techniques taught are knots, anchoring, belaying, rappelling, and climbing. 5 to 1 ratio, less than $50.

Rock I (ratio: 4 to 1, cost: less than $50) continues Basic, with more sustained free-climbing situations. Techniques taught are running belay, multirappel, directional anchors, jamming, and face climbing, up to 5.6 rating.

Advanced courses (ratio: 2 to 1, cost: more than $50)

for learning to lead are offered. Other specialized courses and brochure available.

Lute Jerstad Adventures
P.O. Box 19527
Portland, OR 97219
Director: Lute Jerstad

Jerstad set up the first five-day climbing seminars in the United States and continues to run them today. Offering comprehensive small-group climbing instruction and guide service, Adventures boasts of having some of the best Northwest climbers as instructors. A number of regularly scheduled five-day rock climbing sessions, as well as ice seminars, are held during the summer months for all levels of climbing ability.

Basic classes (cost: about $250) begin with proper balance and proceed to teaching skills of face climbing on small holds and jamming in cracks. Modern quality hardware and ropes are provided. Basic seminars are held at Smith Rock State Park in central Oregon.

Advanced rock seminars (cost: about $250) focus on problems of difficult free climbing, protection on difficult leads, and the art of leading. Guides work on individual problems. Advanced sessions held on granite at Leavenworth Park in central Washington.

Ice climbing sessions (cost: about $300) cover belaying and anchoring and crevass rescue systems, as well as other ice climbing techniques. Write for brochure.

Mt. Rainier Guide Service
Paradise Inn
Mt. Rainier National Park
Paradise, WA
Director: Lou Whittaker

Perhaps having the best reputation in the Northwest, this conservative school offers an experienced staff that teaches twice-weekly, large group ascents and a week-long ice course, among others. Director

Lou Whittaker has done many major climbs and makes sure students are well prepared at the conclusion of the course. Brochure available.

Northern Lights Alpine Recreation
Box 399
Invermere, British Columbia, Canada VOA 1KO
Director: Arnor Larson
   Noted as one of the best climbing schools in North America, Northern Lights offers personalized summer and winter courses in beginning, intermediate, and advanced climbing. Trips are conducted to Selkirks, Bugaboos, Leaning Towers, Assiniboine, and other areas in Alberta and British Columbia. Backpacking trips are also offered. Write for brochure.

International Mountain Climbing School
Box 494
Main Street
North Conway, NH 03860
Director: Paul Ross
   International offers instruction in all aspects of mountaineering, but their most popular courses are their daily beginning, intermediate, and advanced rock and ice climbing classes, held in the White Mountains. Seminars on mountain rescue, and overnight trips and expeditions are also available. The school supplies all equipment except boots. Beginning classes, instruction ratio is 5 to 1; intermediate and advanced, 3 to 1. All classes cost less than $50.

Iowa Mountaineers
P. O. Box 163
Iowa City, IA 52240
Director: Jim Ebert
   The Iowa Mountaineers offers seven-day, basic rock climbing courses at Devil's Lake, Wisconsin, for which

participants can receive college credit. This course includes intensive instruction on the fundamentals of rope management, balance climbing, friction, jam and opposition techniques, belaying, rappelling, down climbing, tension climbing, two-rope bridge crossings, and two and three-person party climbing. Evening lectures cover party makeup and control, philosophy of mountaineering, route selection, leadership, judgment, objective dangers, weather, hypothermia, and equipment care and selection. Color slides illustrate certain discussions. The cost is more than $100. Brochure available upon request.

Recreational Equipment Inc. Climbing School
c/o REI Travel
P. O. Box 22402
Seattle, WA 98122
This school offers various one-day and weekend courses in basic snow and rock climbing through Heather Mountaineering instructors. Weekend trips are limited to six or seven more experienced climbers. Cost is more than $50. One-day trips for inexperienced climbers at Monte Cristo Peak, two hours from Seattle, are less than $50. Full seven-month climbing instruction available to Seattle area residents. Brochure available.

Yosemite Mountaineering School and Guide Service
Curry Village
Yosemite National Park, CA 95389
Director: Loyd Price
Specialists in straight-up rock climbing, Yosemite is one of the best-known schools in America. All day (seven-hour) courses are offered from about Easter until the first week in October, some in the Yosemite Valley, with summer courses in the high country.
An excellently trained staff of experienced instruc-

tors offer basic rock climbing, intermediate I and II, and advanced free-climbing courses. Specialized courses include a snow and ice course, and alpine crest and direct-aid seminars, as well as private or group guided climbs. There are also alpine survival courses.

Class-size ratio is 8 to 1 for beginning and 6 to 1 for intermediate. Prices and brochure available by mail.

Palisades Mountain School
P. O. Box 694
Bishop, CA 93514
Director: John Fisher

Palisades has been in business eighteen years, known by a couple different names (formerly Mountain Travel). Located in the Sierra Nevada's Palisades area near Big Pine, courses run from February to September, taught by a staff of a dozen qualified members. Instruction takes place in small groups (maximum 3 to 1) and courses include basic and advanced rock climbing and a snow and ice course.

Basic rock (ratio: 3 to 1, cost: less than $50) includes holds, body movement, control and relaxation, proper equipment, anchors, rope management, rappelling, and self rescue.

Advanced rock (ratio: 2 to 1, cost less than $50) begins with basic review of safety and climbing skills and progresses in exposure and pace, depending on the level of the students.

Other schools in the United States can be checked by writing for their brochure.

Grand Teton Climbers Ranch
c/o American Alpine Club
113 East 90th Street
New York, NY 10028

Mazamas
909 N.W. 19th Avenue
Portland, OR 97209

Mid-West Mountaineering
309 Cedar
Minneapolis, MN 55454

Potomac Appalachian Trail Club
(Mountaineering Section)
1718 North Street NW
Washington, D.C.

Wolf Creek Wilderness School
Wesser, NC

Also check with the local climbing clubs in your area. Many of them offer instruction at no cost or at a nominal course fee.

6

Learning on Your Own

Books are an alternative way to learn about new techniques or to gain some knowledge of unfamiliar areas of climbing, but they are no substitute for practical, on-the-rock instruction by a qualified instructor. Instead, books should be considered as supplementary sources of learning new climbing skills, or a way to review and expand on those skills already acquired through instruction.

Acquiring new knowledge about climbing is not limited to "how-to" books. One of the books listed here, *Climb*, is a fascinating history of the climbing scene in Colorado and offers a number of instructional tips that are picked up almost by osmosis. The text is very well written and the fascinating historical sagas of climbers put the reader in touch with the vast wealth of effort that has gone into this favorite sport.

Aleith, R. C. *Bergsteigen: Basic Rock Climbing.* Revised ed. New York: Charles Scribner's Sons, 1975. 196 pages (paper), $6.00.

After a very sketchy opening chapter, Aleith settles down to provide some excellent, well-researched, and organized information on climbing. The text is illustrated with some of the best photographs on technique available in any book. The other illustrations are superior as well. The book contains a well-written chapter on all the basics, including face, slab, fissure, down and boulder climbing: rope techniques; piton craft; rappelling; aid climbing; and group climbing.

Godfrey, Bob, and Chelton, Dudley. *Climb!* Boulder, Col.: Alpine House, for American Alpine Club, 1977. 275 pages, $14.95.

This volume, well illustrated with striking black and white photos (some from the "Dark Ages" of climbing) by two experienced climbers, chronicles the gripping tale of rock climbing in Colorado from 1870 to the present. Dividing the historical periods into roughly decade-length segments, the book describes in vivid detail the adventures, dramas, and fiascos of Colorado's most famous climbs and the climbers who did them. Many of the accounts are presented firsthand by the pioneer climbers. There is a great section on the history of bouldering. The work includes more than one hundred fifty photos of spectacular modern rock climbs (you've got to see the shot of Dale Johnson climbing the Third Flat Iron in the 1950s on roller skates), as well as unique, previously unpublished historical photos. *Climb!* is a must for anyone who enjoys either the sport or the history of the old West.

Great Pacific Iron Works Co. *The Great Pacific Iron Works Catalog.* Ventura, Cal. 92 pages (paper) $1.

More a book than a catalog, this inexpensive work

(available from Box 150, Ventura, 93001) contains advice; solid information on climbing; and good photos, essays, and poetry; as well as a description of the company's equipment. Included in the catalog is an excellent article by Doug Robinson called "Running Talus," a good activity for Midwestern climbers, especially at Devil's Lake, Wisconsin. The first Chouinard catalog is now a valuable collectors item. Add this new one to your collection.

Lyman, Tom. *Field Book of Mountaineering and Rock Climbing*. New York: Winchester Press, 1975. 208 pages, $6.95.

This very general book covers the gamut of mountaineering skills. Veteran climber Tom Lyman deals with such topics as moving in the mountains; carrying the gear; tenting; philosophy; specialized footwear; rock climbing; and snow, ice, and glacier travel.

Mendenhall, Ruth and John. *Beginners Guide to Rock and Mountain Climbing*. Harrisburg, Pa. Stackpole, 1975. 159 pages (paper), $3.95.

This is the best book to give the novice a comprehensive overview of the skills and equipment needed to climb rocks and mountains. A well-balanced, systematic body of basic information, presented in a highly readable and well-illustrated style, touches on all the necessary points, though quite briefly in some sections. Excellent for beginners, the book gives a straight forward "how-to" body of knowledge in one quick dose. Many experience-proven tips are given by this husband-and-wife team that has been climbing for more than thirty years.

Mountaineers, ed. *Mountaineering: The Freedom of the Hills*. 3rd ed. Seattle: 1974. 478 pages, $12.95.

This green-cover book is a classic text on general

wilderness mountaineering. The updated version is a good reference work presenting new concepts in equipment, technique and ethics of climbing, and general mountaineering. Its format is a logical progression from the introductory phases of alpine travel to the basic techniques of roped climbing, to the levels of skill required for intermediate and advanced climbing.

Some of the most active and experienced climbers of the Pacific Northwest collaborated on a presentation of modern technique of free and aid climbing, anchoring and belaying, choosing equipment, and what to do after a fall. Rescue procedures, mountain ecology, weather, and mountain travel are discussed in this comprehensive work, well illustrated with photos and excellent line drawings

An excellent section on snow and ice climbing makes this a unique volume that can be considered a basic text on the state of the ar.

Robbins, Royal. *Basic Rockcraft*. Glendale, Cal.: La-Siesta Press, 1971. 70 pages (paper), $2.50.

Written by one of America's foremost climbers, this highly specialized small book touches on all aspects of climbing that novices need to know, including equipment, knots, belaying, direct-aid techniques, nutcraft, rappelling, face climbing, ethics, and style. Although a bit dowdy and the graphics need revision, the book nonetheless is still a classic instruction text for beginners and intermediate climbers.

_____. *Advanced Rockcraft*. Glendale, Cal.: La-Siesta Press, 1973. 95 pages (paper), $3.50.

Taking up where his previous book, *Basic Rockcraft*, leaves off, Robbins has produced a philosophical work on how advanced climbing should be done. Voicing the need for clean climbing as opposed to nailing every aid route, Robbins helped turn the tide of climbers in the cleanliness direction with the introduction of *Advanced Rockcraft*. Much better illustrated than *Basic Rockcraft* (at least one picture every other page), this book is must reading for the climber trying to better his or her technique. The book contains the most comprehensive details of chockcraft yet published. Advanced Rockcraft also covers wall climbing, leading, and solo climbing.

Wheelock, Walt. *Ropes, Knots and Slings for Climbers.* Glendale, Cal: LaSiesta Press, 1967. 36 pages (paper), $1.25.

This small instructional volume, originally published in 1960, is a best seller among climbing texts. The mountaineering rope and knot book was updated by Royal Robbins in 1967 and includes free-climbing rope techniques that continue to lead to first ascents never before thought possible. The many principles of rope handling are still current, making this book as good as ever, but the technology of rope design, construction, and materials has surpassed the information contained in the charts and tables.

Bonus Section:

Bouldering (Or Did You Say "Buildering"?)

Author's Note:

Bouldering is increasing in popularity with climbers, especially in the Midwest. Ready to stand on its own merit as a sport, bouldering is ideally suited to the short, tough cliffs and sheer faces that commonly characterize the Midwestern topography.

"Buildering," a new twist on bouldering, is taking many college campuses and cities by storm. Buildering is the art of bouldering transplanted to the walls of a building, often practiced by the die-hard city-bound "rock jocks" of the college campus, both male and female! Adam Grosowsky, who has written a guidebook to rock climbing areas in Southern Illinois, has contributed the following bonus section on the bouldering/buildering phenomenon that is happening among climbers everywhere in the Midwest. ARB

Bouldering has been called the "poetry of mounaineering." It combines every facet of the sport of rock climbing into a concise, demanding, separate entity. Technically, bouldering is any form of free (unroped and unaided) climbing which terminates as soon as the distance between the climber and the ground becomes dangerously lengthy. For this reason, most boulder problems (as climbers are wont to call them) rarely exceed twenty feet in height and are commonly found on large boulders.

Bouldering encompasses the most difficult end of the rock climbing spectrum. While there are many easy boulder problems, the vast majority are incredibly difficult, requiring much strength and agility. One could almost deem bouldering "rock ballet," a meticulous, planned execution of a series of difficult moves. One is not merely concerned with getting up a problem, but surmounting it with style and grace.

It would seem logical that the sport of rock climbing evolved from bouldering, but in actuality it's the other way around. Bouldering is an offspring from rock climbing which was not really practiced for its own sake until the early 1960s.

During the mid-1960s, Pat Ament and John Gill—among other top name climbers from Colorado—raised the standard of bouldering to new levels. From 1967 to 1969, Ament pioneered such Colorado climbs as First Overhang, Right Side of the Red Wall, The Consideration, and many difficult routes on Capstan Rock. In the company of such experts as Bob Williams, he was able to demonstrate that bouldering had potential as an activity in its own right, rather than merely serving as training for longer climbs.

Ament has called bouldering the "purest from of climbing." "I'm really a boulderer at heart," he once said in a *Summit* magazine article about him. "It's where you find the hardest moves. I like pushing my limits and not having to fiddle with nuts and slings and belays."

Meanwhile, John Gill, a legendary figure among rock climbers, had been acquiring a name for himself as a specialist on extremely difficult technical moves on boulders in the Fort Collins, Colorado, area, particularly face climbs involving minute handholds. In 1968, Ament and Gill met and have bouldered together for years.

Until then, bouldering had been thought of as an exercise, a training measure. A climber merely bouldered to strengthen his forearms and calves, in order to be prepared for the "real" climbing on the higher crags. This attitude was prevalent for quite some time, until climbers started watching or hearing about Gill's phenomenal skill and strength and his untiring devotion to bouldering problems. He transformed bouldering from an occasional training routine to an intensive sport all its own. Gill who has bouldered throughout the United States, was truly a genius before his time. His impact upon contemporary rock climbing cannot be measured, for it was Gill's bouldering techniques and philosophies that fostered the current standards of difficulty in free climbing in America.

Until recently, however, Gill was considered somewhat of an enigma, floating in and out of climbing areas, leaving only bewildered faces and incredible boulder problems behind.

Gill bouldered quite extensively in the Midwest. In Dixon Springs State Park, in the eastern portion of southern Illinois, he tackled quite a number of difficult problems, some of which he wrote about in a magazine article entitled "Climbing Down Home."

Recently, Gill protégé Pat Ament produced an excellent biography of Gill, *Master of Rock*, in which Ament dispels some of the mystery of the elusive Gill, who ten years ago was producing routes far more difficult than many today. *Master of Rock* by Pat Ament is available through Alpine House Publishers, P.O. Box 1763, Boulder, CO 80301. Some Gill trivia: he can (or could) do a one-finger, one-arm pullup with every finger of each hand except the smallest finger. He became so incredibly strong that his ligaments and muscles literally pulled themselves away from the bone, causing repeated layoffs in his climbing. In the Needles of South Dakota, there is a problem called the Thimble, which Gill climbed in the 1960s—the route has never been repeated. These are a few scattered examples that made Gill the most extraordinary boulderer in America.

Bouldering as an art probably also had some of its roots in the proverbial climbers' paradise of Yosemite Valley. In Camp 4, the legendary climbers' "hangout," there are various boulders on which the early "hard men" discovered a multitude of very short, difficult climbs. These often consisted of only one or two moves. Gradually, these boulders became the arena for an innocuous little pastime that became known as bouldering. Climbers resting in camp between long routes on the immense granite walls of the valley often found themselves grunting and swearing on the boulders of Camp 4. So while such names as Clouinard, Harding, Pratt, and Robbins were pounding away at epic ascents, thousands of feet up on the soaring granite, their grounded counterparts strained and contorted on the boulders of the valley floor. These innocent rocks scattered among the dust and pine needles and the climbers assaulting them were the forerunners of modern bouldering and now the second-generation wave of "buildering."

It was Gill again, who devised an addition to the Yosemite Decimal System specifically for bouldering, which pushed the ratings beyond the 5.1 level, at the time the maximum difficulty rating found on long climbs. Since almost all of Gill's routes were more difficult than 5.10, he invented the new designations of B1 and B2 ("B" for boulder). It is safe to say a B1 equals a 5.11 to 5.12, B2 is a 5.12 to 5.13+; because Gill is the only climber to ever have ascended a B3, we will leave that rating up to him.

Bouldering attempts to maximize the sheer physical difficulties of climbing while minimizing the risk. As a sport of its own, it is still primarily used in conjunction with a complete rock climbing schedule, mainly as training to develop forearm and calf muscles. But bouldering also helps sharpen one's mastery of various climbing techniques. It is the essence of climbing, the ultimate in pure difficulty and intimate sensory contact with the rock. It is a common sight in any rock climbing area to see small flocks of climbers congregating at the popular boulders, taking turns falling off some inconsequential little problem—their hands white with gymnastic chalk, their feet bound in tight-fitting rubber rock shoes, and their minds blind with determination.

But now, much more than a training exercise, bouldering instinctively builds route-finding skills and climbers automatically search for weaknesses as they look for linkage between sets of holds. They follow cracks, checking for vulnerabilities. Once this trait is adopted, it becomes virtually impossible to view any material structure without subconsciously assessing its suitability for climbing. Now many landlocked, weather-bound climbers have begun staring at walls of their university buildings or mentally dissecting stone walls and bridges, wistfully tracing plausible routes. These climbers, being resourceful, creative fellows and gals, have done more than wistfully stare. Many climbers, deprived of any natural rock on which to exercise their talents, have turned to bouldering on manmade structures. This new development has opened whole new horizons on the bouldering scene— "Buildering" is coming into its own.

Climbers have been, for the most part, antitechnocratic. They fled to the mountains to escape life's hectic pace and the endless rush of today's technological lifestye. Seeing that escape was inevitably futile, however, the new-breed climber began to roll with the punches. He began to see virtue in a land of architectural vice and decided if you can't beat 'em, join 'em.

The sport of buildering was born and deviates very little from bouldering: The same game, a different board. Instead of granite boulders in the Yosemite sun, its playgrounds are the cement walls bathed in city shadows. The ingenious climber can find superlative "problems" built unintentionally into the everyday architecture. Blocky buildings and stone walls suddenly take on a whole new dimension. Bridge abutments, stone pillars, window ledges—the possibilities are endless. Brick walls with recessed mortar demand superior face-climbing techniques rarely needed in a natural setting. Cracks and chimneys require excellent techniques because of their smoothness.

The builderer acquires an eye for the architecture much as he does for the natural crags. Inverted corners, ledges, holes, cracks, and pillars hide a wealth of possibilities. Buildering is an exercise in creativity in which imagination and ability are your only limitations. Although the moves rarely involve the diverse techniques required on natural rock, they often call for perseverance with one particular technique. Since most modern architecture thrives on continuity and symmetrical order, manmade structures usually demand repetition of one type of move.

For instance, the lie-back corner on a brick or cement building will require mastery of a pure lie-back technique and then demand nothing but repetition of that technique to the top. On a natural route it would

Students from Southern Illinois University at Carbondale starting a buildering problem. Vertical walls are not as easy to climb as they appear. *(SIU Student Newspaper)*

be exceptional to find a single pitch consisting of only one technique. Because buildering stresses pure technique and reinforces that technique through repetition, it insures the diligent builderer of total command over a wide range of techniques. This familiarity with pure technique is an invaluable tool when dealing with difficulties on natural rock.

Another valuable asset acquired from buildering is the ability to devise new techniques when confronted with a situation where existing ascension methods fail. The perfectly vertical nature of most buildings and the profusion of atypical formations often call for new and novel techniques. For many years, the techniques of climbing have been relatively simple. Liebacking, jamming, chimneying, and counter pressure, for instance, could be relied upon to get one up almost any route. As a standard evolved to the present level, however, climbers devised a series of new, exotic techniques in order to cope with the intensity of the modern climb. Complex methods of off-width jamming were developed to deal with the rash of off-width cracks found in Yosemite Valley. An intricate dynamic move, with subtle heel hooks, was invented to surmount large overhangs without resorting to the use of aids. This spirit of ingenuity is especially pronounced in buildering.

Countless incredibly specialized techniques have been formulated to solve an unending stream of difficulties encountered in buildering. This ability to invent new techniques is a priceless advantage to master, as it allows the climber to constantly·expand his or her arsenal of techniques. The beauty of buildering is that one generally looks for moves requiring unconventional techniques. There are innumerable problems demanding new on-the-spot techniques. One important quality inherent in buildering is originality.

The denial of conventional climbing modes is essential. Buildering should add a whole new dimension to the climbing repertoire. One should not necessarily look at a potential building with the conventional eye of a rock climber. Any exercise that will enhance one's climbing ability should be looked at as desirable. Instead of searching for vertical routes of ascension only, the builderer keeps his mind open for any interesting problems that involve climbing skills, such as a pullup contest on a small ledge or a balance contest testing who can walk the farthest on a narrow handrail. Since buildering is already a somewhat synthetic game, installing little rules doesn't detract in the same ethical sense as in pure rock climbing. While these little exercises in the concrete jungle bear little resemblance to their natural counterpart, they exude a certain misplaced charm which gradually seduces the skeptical climber.

A favorite buildering problem on the Carbondale campus of Southern Illinois University indicates how intricate climbing problems can become. The route, a product of Joe Healy's fertile mind, has been responsible for many outbursts of foul language and one broken elbow. The structure is a low ceiling that covers the south entrance to the Student Center. The route starts on a perfectly smooth, square, concrete pillar. Demanding a unique technique, one must ascend ten feet up the pillar to an overhanging ceiling. From here, the climber must negotiate five feet of perfectly horizontal ceiling, using only smooth, square indentations molded into the ceiling. This is a delicate process involving weird counter pressure and odd knee jams. Once the climber reaches the edge of the ceiling, he or

Student Center at SIU offers unique buildering problem with its perfectly horizontal ceiling.

she must gingerly reach over and do a pullup on a three-eights-inch ledge. From here the builderer lunges to a rounded lip on the roof, where the climb ends. This problem, a perfect example of the more advanced end of the building spectrum, indicates the resourcefulness needed to succeed at that level. Don't let this description scare you, however; the vast majority of builderer problems are much easier and one can almost always find a problem correlating to his or her level of skill. One need not be a "rock jock" in order to enjoy buildering.

For an area such as the Midwest, where climbing areas are few and far between, buildering is even more appealing. City-bound climbers can appreciate buildering as an alternative form of entertainment. While the natural environment seems an integral part of the rock climbing game, it is no longer essential. Furthermore, it is rather amazing that one can play the same game, deriving the same gratification, when it is transposed to "artificial turf." And it's conceivable that while buildering is now in a rather whimsical infancy, it could develop into a far more serious sport.

Buildering seems to be a glimpse into tomorrow—a natural progression in the evolution of climbing. When buildering begins to attract more attention, I feel confident it will blossom into a full-fledged sport. Buildering will become another game, with just a small manipulation of the rules. It is a reflection of the "never say die" climbing spirit, a spirit that cannot be dampened by cold cement and steel. It is a new twist and its validity is fast proving itself.

Remember, necessity facilitates invention, so the next time you're caught in the city with the "no-place-to-climb blues, take a look around and don't despair. Adaptation is the key to survival! Quit staring out the window dreaming of clean granite, soaring into a blue California sky. Grab your shoes and climb a building.

Appendix
Equipment Suppliers

The following suppliers offer quality equipment. Catalogs are available upon request.

Camp Trails
3111 W. Clarendon Ave.
P.O. Box 14500
Phoenix, AZ 85063

Climb High
227 Main St.
Burlington, VT 05401

Colorado Mountain
    Industries
Box 44179
Cincinnati, OH 45244

Eddie Bauer
15010 NE 36th
Redmond, WA 98052

1st Lead Mountaineering
Box 94
Telluride, CO 81435

Forrest Mountaineering Ltd.
1517 Platte St.
Denver, CO 80202

The Great Pacific Iron
    Works
P.O. Box 150
Ventura, CA 93001

Himalayan Industries
P.O. Box 5668
Pine Bluff, AR 71601

Hine/Snowbridge
P.O. Box 4059
Boulder, CO 80306

Hirsh Weis (White Stag)
5203 S.E. Johnson Creek
    Blvd.
Portland, OR 97206

International Mountaineer-
    ing Equipment
Box 494
Main Street
North Conway, NH 03860

Jan Sport
Paine Field Industrial Park
Building 336
Everett, WA 98204

Lowe Alpine Systems
1752 North 55th
Boulder, CO 80301

North Face
1234 5th St.
Berkeley, CA 94710

Recreational Equipment Inc.
1525 11th Ave.
Seattle, WA 98122

Seattle Manufacturing Corp.
12880 Northrup Way
Bellevue, WA 98005

Sierra Designs
247 Fourth St.
Oakland, CA 94607

Sportsmen Products
1845 39th St.
P.O. Box 1082
Boulder, CO 80302

Where to Buy Topographic Maps

Topographic maps are a valuable aid in scouting a new climb area. While not absolutely necessary, they often enlighten the really exploratory climber to new areas that may be on private or public property. Since the map indicates terrain features such as cliffs, these maps can lead you to "discover" newly found areas to escape the crowds or to serve as a diversion when you have exhausted all the climbs in this book.

State indexes are available free of charge by writing to the U.S. Geological Survey offices listed here. Ask for current prices and specific ordering information when requesting the index. When ordering directly one of the quadrangles listed under each climb in this book, send in the approximate cost, $2, for each map (overpayments are refunded).

If ordering maps of areas located west of the Mississippi River, send to:

U.S. Geological Survey
Central Region
Box 25286
Denver Federal Center
Denver, CO 80225

If ordering maps of areas located east of the Mississippi River, send to:

U.S. Geological Survey
Eastern Region
1200 South Eads St.
Arlington, VA 22202

Glossary

Aid climbing (also known as direct aid) pitches, moves, or entire climbs where handholds are inadequate to permit free climbing are scaled using pitons, chocks, or expansion bolts, or are fitted with ladder-like slings called etriers for footsteps. Sometimes mechanical ascenders such as Jumars are used to grip the rope.

Anchor a place or device to which one can secure a rope. Can be a piton, chockstone, tree, horn, etc.

Basalt igneous rock type of very fine crystals, very dark in color, often cellular in texture with a dull luster and rich in heavy, iron-bearing minerals such as hornblende, augite, or greenish olivine.

Belay to protect climber from falling (at least very far) by constantly keeping the rope under control.

Bouldering free (unroped) climbing to heights not more than twenty feet.

225

Carabiner   oval-shaped metal snap link with a spring-loaded gate on one side used to clip the climbing rope to another rope, a fixed anchor, or wherever the rope must be securely attached while still allowing it to slide freely.

Chimney   large open crack.

Clean climbing   climbing either free or direct aid, but without the use of pitons, bolts, etc., that would deteriorate the rock. It is generally agreed that the use of chocks is a clean-climbing technique.

Dolomite   Sedimentary rock formed mainly or entirely from limestone by later addition of magnesium. It is commonly light to medium gray or buff colored and is soft (easily scratched by a knife).

Exposure   the climber's awareness of height and the possibility of falling.

Face climbing   ascents made on vertical walls with small but suitable hand and foot holds.

Fissure (crack) climbing   suitable cracks but face climbing is impossible, using jamming, wedging, counterforce, and stemming techniques.

Free climbing   done with aid of chocks, pitons, or other sources of direct aid.

Granite   igneous rock consisting of various minerals equally spaced, with the mineral grains clearly visible. It is massive and hard, made up mainly of quartz and feldspar, but mica or hornblende is common. Exposure at the surface implies extensive uplift and erosion to remove formerly overlying rocks.

Hero Loop   small runners made from 24 to 30-inch lengths of ½ to ⁹⁄₁₆-inch tubular nylon webbing. Made just like standard runner, they are used primarily to tie off partially driven aid pitons.

Pitch   the distance a leading climber ascends before stopping to anchor and belay the second climber up to his stance. Normally this would be a hundred feet or a little more, but can be longer or shorter depending on the type of rock being climbed and the availability of belay stances.

Quartzite very hard, tough, light to medium-colored, metamorphic rock composed mainly of quartz. The granular texture breaks across or through the grains, not around them. Formational events include deposition in water, deep burial and compression, subsequent uplift, and erosion of overlying rocks.

Rappel a means of descent by sliding down a rope. A variety of methods are possible.

Sandstone a sedimentary rock type formed by water or wind deposit, commonly laid down in streams or rivers, along shorelines, and in dunes. Grains of quartz commonly make up sandstone, but it may include other minerals. Stratification is often present.

Slab (friction) climbing large flat rocks with no handholds where climber must rely on friction between the rock and his shoes alone to make upward progress.

Slings small loops of nylon cord or webbing, anywhere from a few inches to several feet in length. Used for rigging anchors or tying into something.

Index